Computers and music

Second edition

R A Penfold

PC Publishing

PC Publishing
4 Brook Street
Tonbridge
Kent TN9 2PJ

Second edition 1992

© PC Publishing

ISBN 1 870775 32 5

British Library Cataloguing in Publication Data

Penfold, R. A.
    Computers and Music: Introduction.
    2 Rev. ed
    I. Title
    780.285

    ISBN 1-870775-32-5

Phototypesetting by Scribe Design, Gillingham
Printed and bound in Great Britain by BPCC Wheatons, Exeter

Preface

Early attempts at getting computers to produce music were, to say the least, of limited success. These first attempts were made using large and quite powerful computers, but they were not intended for this type of application, and were not equipped to produce anything more than a few 'beeps'. Things have certainly changed, and even a small microcomputer plus one or two good electronic instruments can produce some really impressive results. In fact some modern electronic instruments can produce some excellent pieces of music without any external assistance! They can use their built-in computers to produce demonstration pieces which are stored in their memory circuits. Hearing a good demonstration piece of this type will leave you in no doubt about the capabilities of modern electronic musical instruments under computer control. Computer music has certainly 'come of age'.

Probably few musicians now doubt the capabilities of modern computer music anyway. A more likely reason for holding back from this method of music making is jargon and technicalities, which can not be avoided. I would be less than completely honest if I said that using computers to assist in music making does not require any technical knowledge at all. On the other hand, modern microcomputers and many of the programs that run on them, including the vast majority of music software, are designed for the non-computer expert. These programs are designed to be very easy to use, and in many cases the basics of running programs can be mastered in under an hour.

Even with the 'user friendliness' of modern software, the prospective computer music user has a number of hurdles to overcome. You need some basic knowledge about such things as disk drives, the various computers and types of software that are

available, interfaces, and a lot of general information on computers. This information is needed in order to help you buy the right
software and equipment, and to get everything set up correctly.
Also, once the system is up and running, it helps you to avoid
doing something which might seem quite reasonable, but is
actually a silly mistake. Hopefully, this book will provide you with
all the information you require to successfully set up and start
using a computer music system that is well suited to your needs.

Contents

change; In control; In the mode; Pitch wheel; System messages; Song pointer; Song select; Reset; Active sensing; Tune request; System exclusive; Universal system exclusive; Setting up a system.

1 Computer basics

There seems to be a general belief amongst those outside the world of computers that computing is almost entirely concerned with programming. This is a long way from the truth, and probably less than 1% of computer users do a significant amount of programming. This is not really surprising if you give it a little thought. There would seem to be little point in having 99% of computer users producing programs for the other 1% to use! It makes far more sense to have 1% programming and the other 99% actually using the applications programs they produce.

The point here is that a lot of would-be computer users get put off by the prospect of getting deeply involved in programming when there is, in fact, no need for them to get involved in this aspect of computing at all. This is not to say that in order to run applications programs you need no computing technical knowledge at all. A certain amount of technical expertise is needed in order to run a computer system successfully, but only a comparatively limited amount. You will also need to be armed with some knowledge of computers before setting out to buy a system. It is all too easy to make expensive mistakes.

This book is a sort of beginner's guide to computers, but it is aimed primarily at prospective computer users who wish to set up a system for musical applications. I suppose that this mainly means people who would like to set up a computer based MIDI system, but, as we shall see in later chapters, there are a few non-MIDI music applications for computers. Although electronic music has in the past tended to be a rather esoteric pastime with a relatively small following, a combination of MIDI, vast improvements in low cost electronic instruments, and low cost computers has changed the situation completely. There are now large numbers of musicians using electronic instruments, with a fair proportion of these using computer based systems. A lot of musicians who not so long ago would have not given serious thought to setting up an electronic music system are now being tempted by the power of modern systems. No doubt many are being spurred into action by the feeling that they are being left behind.

Hopefully, this book will provide newcomers to computer music systems with all the basic knowledge they need in order to buy, set up, and use a computer music system. It is only fair to point out that electronic music is a pretty vast subject, and studying one book will not make you an expert in every aspect of the business. However, if you progress to the point where you need in-depth knowledge of a particular aspect such as MIDI or synthesis, there are other books in this series which will tell you all you need to know.

QWERTY?

In the world of computer music there are two basic types of keyboard. These are the black and white keyed musical variety, and the so-called 'QWERTY' keyboards. The former presumably requires no elaboration here, but probably few musicians are familiar with the latter. A lot of people seem puzzled by the QWERTY name, but this is simply a reference to the top row of letter keys on a typewriter keyboard. Even if you are fully conversant with a typewriter keyboard, most computer keyboards will probably still be a bit daunting. They generally have a lot more keys than a standard typewriter. For example, the computer keyboard I used to word process this book has some 102 keys, which must be about double that of the standard typewriter.

So just what do all these extra keys do, and why are they necessary? (Figure 1.1) With a typewriter they are unnecessary since you only need to type in number, letters, and punctuation marks. The only extra keys on a typewriter are such things as the spacebar (for inserting spaces between characters) and the shift key. This second key is used to select upper and lower case letters (i.e. capitals and small letters), or in the case of the number keys it selects either numbers or punctuation marks. With the shift key unused you get lower case letters and numbers — with it depressed you get upper case letters and punctuation marks. Usually there is a 'shift lock' key, which operates in a similar manner to the shift key. It is different in that it has a toggle action. In other words, briefly pressing it once has the same effect as

Figure 1.1 The Atari ST computer (top) has the keyboard built into the main unit. The keyboard for the Amstrad PC1512 (lower) is a separate unit.

holding down the shift key. Pressing it again is like releasing the shift key, pressing it a third time is like holding down the shift key again, and so on.

Another extra key is the backspace key, which simply moves back one character at a time so that corrections can be made. Most typewriters have some form of 'tab' (tabulation) key. This advances the carriage to preset points in a line. For example, it it quite common to have the first tab-stop five or ten characters in from the left hand margin. The tab key is then used to advance the carriage to the correct starting point for indented paragraphs, rather than having to press the spacebar five or ten times.

Cursor

A computer keyboard is normally based very closely on a standard typewriter type, and these extra keys are normally present. They may differ slightly in the way that they function though. The most

3

obvious difference is that the backspace key normally deletes characters as it moves the 'cursor' back along a line. It is important to understand the concept of a cursor, since there are few programs which do not make use of one in some form or other. Remember that with a computer you are not normally producing hard copy straight onto paper. What you type in almost invariably appears on the screen of a monitor, or a television screen used instead of a monitor. The cursor is simply an on-screen character of some kind which shows where the next character you type will appear on the screen. Cursors come in all shapes and sizes, but for a text application such as word processing it is normally something quite simple. In the case of the word processor I use it is in the form of a flashing underline character. Cursors are often made to flash on and off a couple of times per second. This makes them easier to find amongst a screen-full of text. It is not uncommon for the user to be able to choose from a range of several available cursors.

Being able to easily delete and correct mistakes on-screen is one of the great advantages of computers over more traditional methods of producing printed documents. You get things right and then you commit them to paper using a printer. With most programs it is simple to make large alterations to the work you are producing. This contrasts with the difficulties in making even minor changes using conventional paper and ink methods.

You are not limited to simply deleting backwards until an error has been obliterated. Using the cursor keys you can move the cursor to any desired point on the screen, and then add and (or) delete anything (provided the computer and software support this full screen editing feature). There are four cursor keys which are marked with arrows pointing to the left, right, up and down. The arrows indicate the direction in which each of the cursor keys moves the cursor. They simply move the cursor — they do not delete anything or alter what has been typed onto the screen unless they are used in conjunction with other keys.

Something that often causes confusion is the inclusion of both a backspace key and one marked 'del' (short for delete). Exactly how these two keys operate depends on the computer in use and the software it is running. The most common arrangement is for the backspace key to move the cursor back one space and delete the character at its new screen position. The delete key normally deletes the character above the cursor (if there is one) and does not alter the position of the cursor.

Just scrolling

Computer displays have steadily improved over the years, but it is probably true to say that this is still one of the weakest aspects of most computers. The resolution of both text and graphics screens is usually very limited, and even most so-called high resolution screens do not permit very large amounts of information to be shown on-screen at any one time. To some extent the same is true of paper and printing. If you wish to put large amounts of information down on paper, whether it is a novel or a musical score, you use numerous pieces of paper to do it.

The same paging technique can be used with computers, with screens of information being used instead of pages of paper. However, this does not normally operate on the basis of a new blank screen being displayed once a screenfull of information has been produced. Virtually all software that can operate with multiple screens of information seems to operate using a system of scrolling. In other words, when you reach the bottom of the screen, all the text moves up by one line. This gives you a new blank line at the bottom of the screen, while the top line is scrolled off the top of the screen. This does not mean that the top line is lost; you can scroll it back onto the screen again using the cursor keys, but the bottom line will then be lost off the screen.

In practice there could be hundreds of lines of text stored in the computer, but only one block of (typically) 25 lines would be shown on the screen at any time. Using the cursor keys, plus possibly some other keys to permit rapid jumps, you can move to any part of the text so that it can be checked and edited. Many systems are not only limited to this vertical scrolling. Say you wish to produce a document that has a maximum line length of some 120 characters, but the screen of your computer can only display a maximum of 80 characters per line. Horizontal scrolling could be used to give the required 120 characters per line, but with only an 80 character wide portion being displayed on the screen at one time.

This system of scrolling is not confined to text applications, and it is also used with some graphics applications. In a musical context, a common application of scrolling would be in a score writer or notation program. These are different names for the same type of program, which is one for producing printed musical scores. A sort of note processor if you like. A typical arrangement would have staves that scrolled left and right to permit a large number of bars to be included in the score. With the more simple systems the maximum number of staves would be governed by the resolution of the screen and the maximum number that its vertical resolution permitted. With more sophisticated systems you are allowed something like a maximum of sixteen or thirty two staves, but with perhaps only five or six being displayed on the screen at once. Vertical scrolling is used to select the particular block of five or six staves that you wish to work on.

A convenient way of regarding this arrangement is with the text or whatever on a giant piece of paper. The monitor gives a window through which any part of the paper can be viewed, and the cursor keys provide a means of moving the paper so that the area of the paper you wish to see is visible through the monitor's screen. It has to be said that the small amount of the electronic paper that the monitor enables you to see can be a bit awkward and limiting. On the other hand, computers usually bring such massive advantages that it is well worthwhile putting up with this drawback. When moving over to a computer based system you need to accept the fact that it will take some time to adjust to the new way of doing things. After you have gained some experience, and provided you are using well designed software, you should find that operating the system has become intuitive. You will probably wonder how you ever managed to do things any other way!

Computerly functions

Not all computers have function keys, but I have not encountered any recent machines that lack this feature. There are usually eight, ten, or twelve of these, marked f1, f2, etc. These have no conventional typewriter counterparts, and their precise purpose varies from one program to another. When running some software on a computer they might actually have no effect at all. The way in which they are used is entirely up to the programmer.

A typical application of function keys would be to provide the additional features that a word processor has when compared to a typewriter. For instance, with most word processors you can have the right hand margin justified (i.e. all complete lines of text taking up the full line, with additional spaces being added by the computer to pad-out lines where necessary), or the right hand margin can be left ragged. Function key 1 could be used to toggle this feature on and off. As another example, function key 2 could be used to send a document out to the printer. Taking a music oriented application for function keys, in a notation program these could be used to select note values which would then be placed onto the on-screen staves. Some programs are supplied together with a plastic template which fits around the function keys and indicates their purpose.

Other keys which have no typewriter equivalent are the 'Ctrl' (control) and 'Alt' (alternative) keys. Once again, these are not present on all computer keyboards, but seem to be included on all the recent keyboards I have seen. Used on their own they do not usually have any effect at all. They are really a form of shift key, and are normally used in conjunction with one or more of the character keys. For example, instead of using the function keys to access the various functions the programmer might implement a system that uses various letter keys in conjunction with the Alt and Ctrl keys. Taking our earlier example of a word processor and switching its justification on and off, pressing Ctrl and the J key could be used as an alternative to a function key. This method of control can be very easy to use if it is implemented sensibly. Ctrl and J (for justification) is a lot easier to remember than something like f5.

The Ctrl and Alt keys do not have to be used as an alternative to function keys, and can be used in conjunction with them. With the word processor I use the various functions of the program are accessed by using the function keys either in isolation, or in conjunction with either the shift, Ctrl, or Alt keys. Thus each of the ten function keys can be used to access four separate functions, giving a total of forty functions. For a complex program this method is a good one in that it permits the required number of functions to be implemented. It is inconvenient in that it is difficult to learn the key combinations that give the functions you require. Some form of function key template becomes virtually essential with this method of control.

Keypads

Most computer keyboards seem to sport a numeric keypad. This is merely a calculator style keypad which is easier to use than the QWERTY keyboard when a lot of numeric data must be entered into the computer. Some computers, notably some IBM PCs and compatibles, have a combined keypad and cursor key cluster. Normally the 8, 6, 2 and 4, keys on the pad function as the up, right, down and left cursor keys. However, operating the 'Num Lock' keys causes them to operate as number keys. Pressing 'Num Lock' again sets these keys back to cursor operation. This method did not prove to be very popular with computer users, and the more recent IBM PCs and compatibles seem to have a separate cursor key cluster (although the numeric keypad can still be set to cursor key operation if desired).

In the days of mechanical typewriters a lever was used to pull the carriage back to the beginning of the line and advance the paper down onto the next line. With the advent of electric and electronic typewriters this was replaced with a 'Return' key which automatically provided this function when pressed. Computers also have a Return key, although it is sometimes called by the alternative name of the 'Enter' key. Of course, its effect is to move the cursor down the screen by one line and to the beginning of that line.

Great escape

Virtually all computer keyboards are equipped with an 'Esc' (Escape) key. This is another example of a key that does not have a well defined purpose, and which tends to operate slightly from one computer to another, and from one program to another. However, its normal use is to cancel a function that you selected by mistake. Say you start printing out a long document and suddenly realise that you have made an error which must be corrected before the document is printed. It would be wasteful of both time and paper to let the computer print out the whole document, then correct it, and finally print out the corrected version. Usually the Esc key would enable you to prematurely exit from a facility such as the print one, or there will be some other key or combination of key presses that would enable you to do so. My advice would be to avoid programs which do not permit this type of quick escape. They are likely to be difficult and frustrating to use.

On some computers there are some keys which seem to be little used in practice. On my Dell System 200 computer's keyboard there are keys such as 'Alt Gr' and 'Pause' which I have never used. The manuals for applications software should give details of exactly what keys such as these do (if they are not mentioned then they almost certainly have no effect whatsoever with the programs concerned).

WIMPs

A common criticism of early computer software was that it was difficult to learn and use. This led to a great deal of effort to produce programs that performed complex tasks but were easy to learn and operate. In computer terminology, much effort was put into making programs user friendly. There is more than one way of tackling this problem, and many computer users are of the opinion that the best way to make a program user friendly is to sell it together with a really good manual. Computer and software manuals, in general, are not noted for being particularly easy to follow! A good manual is certainly an asset for any program, but it is not really a complete answer to user friendliness.

A well written program can render the manual virtually unnecessary, and most programs that fall into this 'very user friendly' category make use of the WIMP environment. WIMP is an acronym, and it stands for 'Windows − Icons − Mouse − Pointer' (Figure 1.2). If we take each of these in turn, a window is merely an area of the monitor's screen which is given over to a particular task. With a word processor for instance, it might be

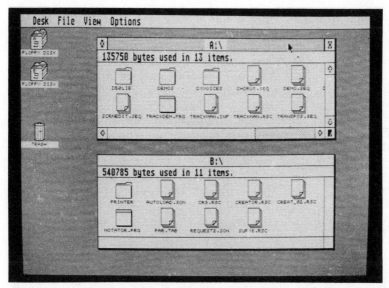

Figure 1.2 A screen shot showing a WIMP environment. This is GEM on the Atari ST, with windows showing the contents of the disks in drives A and B

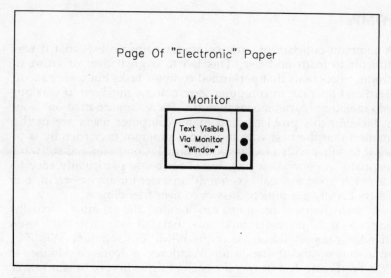

Figure 1.3 Many programs use the monitor as a window which can effectively be moved around a large page of text and/or graphics

possible to edit two documents at once, with each having its own window. Taking a musical application, a notation program could have one window for the staves, and another one for setting up such things as the time signature, key signature, etc.

There is no limit to the number of windows a program can have, but in practice the screen resolution sets a limit on the number of windows that can usefully be utilized. With a lot of windows they are inevitably rather small, and each one can only display a very limited amount of information. Just how windows are handled depends on the program in question. You might have a screen with two or three windows of fixed size. With a true WIMP environment it is possible to switch windows on and off, resize them, and move them around the screen. In practice few applications programs provide quite this degree of flexibility, or need it, but some control over the size of windows is often possible.

An Icon is merely an on-screen representation of something. In a musical applications program you might have a built in metronome function, and this could be switched on and off via a little on-screen drawing of a metronome, or a metronome icon in computer terminology.

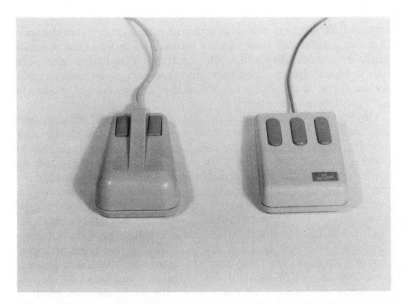

Figure 1.4 Two- and three-button mice. The Amstrad mechanical type (left) and the Mouse Systems optical type (right)

A fair question at this stage is how do you manipulate the icons? This is achieved using the mouse and the on-screen pointer that it controls. The mouse (Figure 1.4) is simply a small plastic box which is moved around on the desk top, or on its special mouse pad. Moving the mouse left, right, backwards and forwards respectively moves the on-screen pointer left, right, down and up. The mouse is equipped with one, two or three push button switches. The purpose of each switch depends on the particular computer concerned, and possibly on the applications program as well.

One of the buttons is used for 'clicking' on icons. In other words, you manipulate the mouse to position the pointer over the desired icon, and then briefly press the push button switch once (which will produce the clicking sound from which the term is derived). In some cases a single click only causes the icon to be highlighted in some way to show that it has been selected, and 'double-clicking' (i.e. pressing the push button switch twice) is necessary in order to make something happen.

Virtually any action a computer program can provide can be selected using icons and clicking. For instance, with a notation program you could select the length of note to be entered onto the

11

stave by clicking on one of a series of note icons. I stated earlier that the pointer can take various forms, and in this case it would probably assume the shape etc. of the selected note icon. The mouse would then be used to position the note at the desired point on the stave, and clicking on one of the buttons would 'paste' the note in place on the stave.

Obviously clever and imaginative use of a WIMP environment can make applications programs very easy to use. It is often possible to learn much about using programs of this type just by playing around with them for a while, and only occasional consultations of the manual might be needed. On the other hand, this means of handling program control is not necessarily a particularly fast one. Learning large numbers of keyboard control codes can be very time consuming initially, but can permit very fast operation of a program once the learning process has been completed and you have become proficient at using the program.

Many applications programmers recognise this, and provide dual control. All or most of the program's facilities can then be accessed by the mouse via icons, or via the keyboard. You can then quickly get to grips with the program initially by using the mouse and icons, but can take the keyboard shortcuts to speed thing up once you become more familiar with the program. A combination of mouse and keyboard control often proves to be the most satisfactory. If you encounter a program that permits only mouse control, and it is one that you are likely to use for a number of hours per week, you would need to think very seriously about how usable it will be in the long term. To a large extent this depends on personal preference, and just how much data etc. you will need to enter into the program.

On the menu

Menus are not an essential part of a WIMP environment, but you would be hard pressed to find a WIMP based program that does not make extensive use of them. A problem with accessing every facility of a program via the mouse and icons is that a large number of icons are likely to be needed, and it is unlikely that there will be sufficient display area to accommodate them all. In order to overcome this problem it is common practice for the frequently used facilities to be accessed by way of icons, with menus being used for the less frequently used facilities.

A menu is merely a list of options that appears on the monitor's screen. In its most basic form there are several numbered options listed, and you press the number key for the particular option you require. Menus that are part of a WIMP system are almost invariably of the 'pop-down' or 'pull-down' varieties. With these methods there is a menu bar across the top of the screen, and this is just a series of headings which identify each of the available menus. You select one of these by placing the pointer on it and either clicking or 'dragging'. Dragging differs from clicking in that instead of briefly pressing the push button switch, it is held down. Dragging can also be used to move things around the screen in some cases, and it is from this that the name is derived.

If we consider pop-down menus first, having clicked on the menu bar the appropriate menu drops down from beneath its heading word. You then move the pointer down onto the required heading and click on it. The function you have selected is then activated. If you wish to exit from a menu without selecting an option it is usually possible to do so by pressing a certain key on the keyboard, or by moving the pointer onto a blank area of screen outside the menu and clicking. Moving the pointer onto a new heading on the menu bar and clicking will usually activate the newly selected menu and close the previously selected one.

With a pull-down menu pressing on the push button switch and keeping it depressed results in the required menu appearing beneath the heading word. The mouse is then used to move the pointer down to the required menu option, and it is then selected by releasing the push button switch. If no menu option is required after all, simply move the pointer off the menu area and release the push button switch.

With both types of menu it is normal for the currently selected option to be shown in reverse video (which is also known as inverse video). In other words, instead of having black lettering on a white background, the currently selected option is shown in white lettering on a black background. This makes it perfectly clear which option is currently selected, and helps to avoid time consuming (and potentially disastrous) errors.

Screen resolution

Screen resolution is a topic that was covered briefly earlier in this chapter, and it is worth considering it in more detail here. Figures for screen resolution can be a little confusing as they are expressed differently for text and graphics screens. A screen resolution with fairly low figures such as 80 × 25 would refer to the text resolution of a display. It merely means that there is a maximum of 80 characters per line, with up to 25 lines per screenfull.

Many music applications programs make use of graphics, and it is then the graphics resolution that is of more importance. A lot of computers have a maximum graphics resolution of 320 × 200 (or 320 × 256) in four colours, or 640 × 200 (or 640 × 256) in two colours. A graphics screen is made up from small dots known as 'pixels'. A screen resolution such as 320 × 256 simply means that the display is formed from 320 dots across the screen, and there are 256 lines of 320 pixels down the screen. Obviously, the higher the horizontal and vertical resolutions, the greater the amount of information that can be displayed. A resolution of 320 × 200 or 256 is not really very good, and the results tend to be rather 'chunky' with the individual pixels being clearly visible. Four colours is not quite as good as it sounds either, since the background colour counts as one of the four colours. However, three foreground colours plus the background colour is adequate for most music applications. Some computer displays do not permit much choice when it comes to the palette of four colours, and this can result in some rather gaudy screens.

Much music software does not benefit greatly from the use of colour, and a higher resolution monochrome display will often give better results. Note that a two colour screen mode is a monochrome type, as the two colours are the background and foreground colours (not the black background and two foreground colours).

It seems to be unusual for eight bit computers (such as the Amstrad CPC range and the Commodore 64 series) to offer screen resolutions beyond those mentioned above. However, most sixteen bit machines (such as the Commodore Amiga, Atari ST and IBM PC series) seem to offer higher resolution and more colour. The Atari ST series, for example, offers three display modes. The medium resolution mode is much used for music software, and this has 640 × 200 pixels with up to four colours. The high resolution mode is probably more popular with music users though, and this offers 640 × 400 pixels in monochrome.

There are various display adaptors available for the IBM PC range, including some which offer quite high resolutions (800 × 600 in sixteen colours not being untypical these days). There is little (if any) music software which makes use of these high resolution modes though, and to take full advantage of them you really need a large monitor or very good eyesight! The standard EGA (enhanced graphics adaptor) with its 640 × 350 resolution in sixteen colours is better supported, and can provide superb results.

The difference between a screen resolution of (say) 320 × 200 and 640 × 400 is greater than you might think. With 640 × 400 resolution it is possible to display four 320 × 200 screens. In terms of what can be displayed in a music context, if a notation program could display three bars on four staves at the lower resolution, it would be able to display six bars on eight staves at the higher resolution. The importance of high screen resolution depends very much on the software you will be running, and how much you will need to display at once in order to render the program really usuable. Bear in mind though that even a resolution of about 640 by 400 does not let you display a great deal, and may take some getting used to. Even a modest score would occupy a large number of screens. High resolution generally costs significantly more when buying a computer system, but for music applications programs it will usually be money well spent.

The system

So far we have only considered a computer system as a keyboard and an optional mouse which are used to enter information into the system, and a monitor which displays the results of your efforts. You may simply prefer to leave things at this level and not delve any deeper into the inner workings of a computer. However, a basic understanding of how a computer operates can bring practical benefits. Most of the time it is possible for computer users to get by with no technical knowledge, but this does leave open the possibility of making silly mistakes that could be avoided with the aid of a little more knowledge about how things work. You may prefer to skip over this next section, but it would be sensible to at least quickly read it through.

If looked at in the most simple possible terms a computer system breaks down into the arrangement shown in Figure 1.5. Here the keyboard and the monitor are the main means of getting information into and out of the computer. They have been discussed in some detail previously in this chapter, and will not be considered further here.

The microprocessor is the device at the heart of the system. This controls everything else in the system, either directly or with the aid of special electronic circuits. Although the microprocessor tends to be regarded as the brain at the centre of things, this is

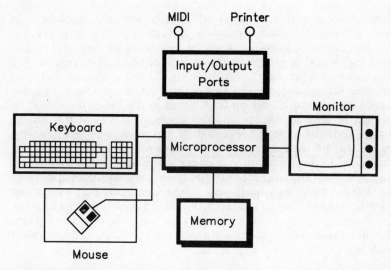

Figure 1.5 The basic stages which make up a computer. The microprocessor is very much at the heart of things

perhaps flattering it slightly. It does not decide what it must do, but simply follows the instructions it finds in the memory section of the system. This is where the applications program is loaded by the user, and then executed by the microprocessor. It is a gross oversimplification to suggest that the microprocessor simply follows the instructions in the memory circuits when the program is run. If this was the case, the effect of running the program would be the same every time it was run. Much of the time the microprocessor is simply looping indefinitely, waiting for some input from the user via the keyboard or a mouse. It then acts upon that information using the appropriate instructions stored in memory.

Most programs actually consist of the main program which monitors the keyboard and awaits input from the user, and a series of sub-programs which are called up by the main program. If you wish to print something out, then the printing sub-program is called up. If you want to enter notes onto the stave of a notation program, then the note entering program is called up by the main program. Software tends to be quite complex these days, and sub-programs might even call up sub-sub-programs. This method of writing software helps to keep things manageable for the software writers. Most complex applications programs are actually written by a small team of programmers, and this approach makes things easier with the committee approach to software production. It can bring advantages to the user as well. Software that it written in a sensible and well ordered manner is almost invariably much better to use than software which has been written in a haphazard fashion with lots of features tagged on here and there.

The computer's memory is not just used for storing program instructions. It is also used for storing data. This includes data that is supplied with the program, and which the program needs in order to do tasks such as producing the initial screen display. In many applications a substantial proportion of the computer's memory is given over to the storage of data supplied by the user. In a musical context programs are often required to store music in one form or another. It might be in the form of MIDI data supplied from a synthesizer, or music entered into a notation program from the computer keyboard or mouse. In either case anything more than a very brief and simple piece is likely to require a substantial amount of memory. As music programs tend to be quite complex and the user often supplies vast amounts of data, many musical applications for computers are only a practical proposition on a machine that is well endowed with memory.

Ins and outs

While the keyboard and monitor represent the primary means of getting information into and out of most computers, there are normally other routes. The input/output ports of a computer accommodate peripheral devices such as the mouse and a printer. For music applications there would often be some means of communicating with electronic musical instruments, which these days almost always means MIDI input and output ports. Input/output ports and peripherals equipment are an important aspect of computing, and one which is considered in detail in Chapter 3.

The processor

I suppose that for many non-technical computer users the microprocessor tends to be regarded as a mysterious device. You provide instructions to the computer and it acts upon them to do all sorts of wonderful things. In most cases it seems to do those things at an almost unbelievable speed. Microprocessors are undeniably complex components, containing the equivalent of tens of thousands of electronic components, and in some cases having the equivalent of a few hundred thousand components. Their internal circuits contain so many parts that even with each one consuming only minute power levels, the overall level of power consumption is such that these components usually run very hot indeed. In fact the microprocessor in the computer I use for word processing is fitted with an electronic metal cooling fin. Without this it would overheat and be destroyed after a few minutes of operation.

Although microprocessors are very complex devices, much of the processing they undertake is really quite simple. Also, by general electronic standards they are not particularly fast in operation. They manage to perform quite impressive tasks by virtue of the fact that they still operate quite fast in human terms, performing in excess of one million instructions per second in some cases. Even if each instruction achieves very little, with this rate of through-put many tasks can be performed at a speed which appears to be instant to the operator. Also, most computers have a lot of electronics to back up the microprocessor so that it can get on with the more important tasks and not get overloaded with the more mundane chores. In particular, there are usually complex devices to handle tasks such as the generation of the video display, and interfacing to other peripheral devices such as the keyboard, printer, MIDI instruments, etc.

It is not uncommon for there to be microprocessors in one or more of these peripheral controller circuits. Keyboards often contain a dedicated microprocessor, and they are occasionally to be found in video display generator circuits. Probably the main factor in modern software performing as well as it does is the ingenuity of the best programmers. Looking at the hardware in some popular microcomputers, and the functions they perform when running the best programs available, quite frankly it is difficult to see how they manage it!

Sequencing

It is perhaps easier to understand the type of processing undertaken by a microprocessor if we consider a practical example, albeit in highly simplified terms. Probably the most common musical application for a computer is as a MIDI sequencer. The computer functions as what could be regarded as a sort of tape recorder.

However, instead of recording sounds from the instrument, it records data from the MIDI output socket of the synthesizer. The system as a whole operates as what is really more akin to a player-piano than a tape recorder, since the only way of replaying a sequence is for the computer to feed the recorded data back into the synthesizer via its MIDI input socket.

The output from a MIDI instrument is a series of numbers in digital form. You do not really need to understand in detail the way in which numbers are converted into digital form — it is basically just a matter of switching a small electrical current on and off at high speed. Each pattern of on/off switching represents a number between 0 and 255, and the output from a MIDI keyboard is no more than a series of numbers in this range. Obviously the numbers have meanings, and those above 127 are codes which indicate such things as a note to be switched on or off, or a change to the modulation depth. Numbers of 127 and less are used to carry data, such as which particular note must be switched on or off, how hard a key has been struck, and so on. Some MIDI messages just consist of one number in the 0 to 255 range (or one 'byte' in computer terminology), but most consist of a message code byte followed by one or two data bytes. For example, it takes three bytes to switch on a note, and another three to switch it off again.

The basic action of a MIDI sequencer is for the microprocessor to wait for values to be received on the MIDI input, and to store them in a block of memory. The MIDI input hardware can either produce a signal (known as an 'interrupt') to tell the microprocessor that a new value has been received, or the microprocessor must repeatedly monitor a 'flag' in the MIDI hardware until it detects that a fresh value is ready to be read. The microprocessor uses a few bytes of memory to act as a counter to indicate where in memory the next value must be stored. In computer jargon, the counter indicates the next memory 'address' to be used to store a received value. This ensures that no values are over-written by subsequent values, and that the MIDI data can be recovered from memory in the correct order.

The values on their own are of little use as they lack the all-important timing information. A microprocessor can easily provide electronic timing, but most computers have at least one timer circuit which the microprocessor can use to time the gap between one byte of MIDI data and the next. This timing information is stored away in the computer's memory together with the received MIDI data.

Playing back the MIDI data is just a matter of the microprocessor transferring the first value in memory to the MIDI output port, then taking the first timing value. The computer's timer is then monitored until the appropriate time has elapsed, after which the second value in memory is transferred to the MIDI output port. The next piece of timing information is then taken from memory, the computer's timer is monitored until the appropriate time has elapsed, the next value is sent to the MIDI output, and so on until all the values in memory have been transmitted.

This is all very simple, and a basic real-time sequencer is the type of thing that even a beginner at programming could probably produce without too much difficulty. Commercial sequencer software goes well beyond this basic record/playback facility though. A standard feature is the ability to alter the playback speed of a sequence. This type of thing has drastic consequences with conventional tape recording due to the changes in pitch that are produced, but with MIDI sequencing the tempo can be altered without any corresponding shift in pitch on the played-back music. Changing the tempo is not difficult to achieve with the aid of the microprocessor's mathematical capabilities. One way of implementing this facility is to multiply all the timing values in memory by a suitable amount (using a value of more than one to reduce the tempo, or a value of less than one in order to increase it). A better method is to provide the mathematical manipulation on each timing value during the playback process, after reading it from memory. This still gives the required effect, but leaves the data in memory unaltered (known as 'non-destructive' editing).

Another common feature is multi-tracking. In other words, after recording one track, another one can be recorded alongside it. The two can then be played back as a single piece of music, just like multi-tract tape recording. Also like multi-track tape recording, large numbers of tracks can be laid down side by side and played back together if required. The recording process is quite simple, and is not much different to that of a basic single track sequencer. The only slight difficulty is in ensuring that one track does not over-write memory that has already been used for an existing track.

The playback process is a bit more difficult, as data for perhaps as many as two or three dozen tracks must be monitored and merged together into a single output. This is a more complex task, but is one that is within the capabilities of most microprocessors. However, this sort of thing can take a lot of processing, and large numbers of notes spread over dozens of tracks could overload the more simple microprocessors, or the better ones if the software is anything less than well written.

A whole range of features can easily be added to a sequencer. MIDI makes use of a channelling system with the channel number contained in the message type bytes. This enables a track to be directed to just one of several instruments in a system, or even just one voice of a particular instrument in the system. With most sequencers you do not need to record each track on the MIDI channel it must be transmitted on. You use any channel when recording and then set the transmission channel to whichever one you require with the aid of the sequencer's channel setting controls. Microprocessors have simple decision making instructions which work along the lines of 'if the first number is the same as the second one then do this, or if it is not then do that instead'. This type of thing can be used to determine which bytes contain channel numbers, and to change channel numbers to the required values where necessary.

Data shuffling

When told that basically all a microprocessor does is to shuffle numbers around from one part of the system to another, and provide a little mathematical manipulation and simple decision making where necessary, most non-computer buffs do not believe it. As should be apparent from the above description of how sequencing is accomplished, this really is all that a microprocessor does! Although microprocessors seem to do very clever things, the situation is a bit deceptive They are very impressive in situations where real-world things can be converted into numbers that the microprocessor can process, and then convert back into real-world things again. Preferably both conversion processes should be fairly simple.

Microprocessors are less impressive at tasks where real world things can not be easily digitized, or produce enormous quantities of complex digital data. We can recognise people from their faces with little difficulty, and can even tell a lot about their moods from the expressions on their faces. Microprocessors need a lot of interfacing hardware to do this type of thing at all, and provide less than impressive results. It takes some clever programming before they can even distinguish between the face and the background.

Fortunately for musicians, data from musical instruments is easily digitized, and is readily digestible by microprocessors. This enables relatively low cost hardware and software to provide some very powerful facilities.

2 Storage media

Methods of storing computer data and programs were touched on briefly in the previous chapter. This is an important aspect of computing, and it is one which is well worth considering in detail in a chapter of its own. When running complex programs, which includes most music applications types, it is surprising how much difference it can make if the storage facilities of a computer are upgraded. Programs that were previously slow and cumbersome to use suddenly operate much more quickly and easily. Perhaps of even greater importance, some programs will only run on a computer that has a substantial amount of memory and high capacity disk drives. Before buying any program you need to ensure that it will actually run on the particular configuration you are using.

RAM

You can not look at computer advertising literature for long without coming across the term RAM. In fact several popular computers have a number in their name which indicates the amount of RAM they are endowed with. The Commodore 128 for example, has 128k of RAM. RAM stands for 'random access memory', but this term is a bit misleading. All the memory devices I have encountered have had the facility to access any memory cell at any time, or this so-called 'random access' facility. What really distinguishes RAM from other types of memory is that the computer can alter its contents. When a computer is first switched on the applications program is normally loaded from disk (or whatever) into the computer's RAM.

Any data produced by the user is initially loaded into RAM. There is a severe drawback with ordinary RAM devices in that they

23

suffer from instant amnesia as soon as the computer is switched off. In computer terminology RAM is 'volatile' memory. Consequently, RAM is no use for long term or even medium term storage of data. Before you switch off the computer any important data held in RAM must be stored on some more permanent medium, which usually means a computer disk of some kind. When working on a large project that will involve hours of work it is normal to save data in RAM to disk every half an hour so that, in the event of an accidental power loss, hours of hard work is not totally lost. You can load in the latest version of the work on disk, and will have lost what will probably be no more than a few minutes work.

It has to be admitted that the risk of losing work due to a computer fault is a definite drawback of computers. On the other hand, it is one that can easily be exaggerated, and often is. Having used computers for many hours per week for nearly ten years now, the amount of work that I have lost amounts to what is probably only about one or two hours' worth. While this is unfortunate, it is vastly outweighed by the thousands of hours I have saved. Also, a lot of the projects I have undertaken I would probably not have attempted if is was not for my computerized help. Do not overlook the fact that work produced by more conventional means is also vulnerable. If someone spills a cup of coffee over the hand written score for your latest song it could take a long time to get it accurately copied out again. If someone spills coffee over a computer print out you merely get the computer to produce another copy.

You may occasionally come across references to 'non-volatile' RAM, or 'battery-backed' RAM. This is where a computer (or other item of electronic equipment) has some memory which does not lose its contents when the equipment is switched off. True non-volatile RAM does not lose its contents as it uses some form of storage cell which will remain unaltered by the removal of the power source. It therefore takes up exactly where it left off when the power is restored. This type of RAM has never received widespread use, probably because RAM devices of this type are far more expensive than conventional types.

Battery-backed RAM is the more normal solution, and this makes use of ordinary RAM chips that have a very low current consumption under standby conditions. A battery is used to maintain power to the RAM chips when the main supply is switched off, and due to the low power consumption of the RAM chips this battery will last for months or even years. In some cases the battery is actually included 'on-board' each RAM component, with a guaranteed lifespan of about five years. It is more normal though, to have a separate battery supply which must be replaced from time to time.

Another arrangement is to have a nickel-cadmium rechargeable battery to provide the back-up supply. This is automatically recharged when the main supply is present. Therefore, provided the computer is not left unused for long periods of time, the back-up battery supply for the RAM will remain present until the batteries can no longer retain a charge. This usually means five years or more of trouble-free operation.

I would not like to give the impression that there are a lot of computers which have their main RAM battery-backed, or use non-volatile RAM for all their RAM. I have used a large number of different computers, but have yet to encounter any that have any non-volatile RAM at all. I have used several computers which have battery-backed RAM, but only a very small percentage of the total RAM was of this type (less than 0.01% in fact). The standard use of battery back-up is to maintain power to a built-in clock/ calendar circuit so that you do not have to enter the time and date into the computer each time you use it. A small amount of RAM is also battery-backed so that it can supply information to the computer at switch-on. This information can be configuration details for the particular setup in use (how much main memory, number and type of disk drives, etc.), or in some cases it can be data to start up the computer in the desired screen mode, and things of this type. Incidentally, battery backed RAM is often used in synthesizers to store data for preset and user defined sounds. This avoids having to readjust hundreds of parameters each time the instrument is switched on, or having to load the sound data from tape to disk.

By no means all computers have any battery backed RAM, and it is a comparative rarity amongst home computers. It is fairly standard on computers which are primarily intended for business use.

Static or dynamic

Terms which sometimes puzzle newcomers to computing are 'static' RAM and 'dynamic' RAM. Static RAM is the type which is used in battery-backed RAM systems. It does not lose its contents if it is left unused for long periods of time, and it has the all-important feature of a low current consumption under standby conditions. Dynamic RAM loses its contents unless it receives the attention of 'refresh' circuits. This means that it will only retain its

25

contents while some other parts of the computer are operational, and it can not achieve the very low levels of current consumption associated with static RAM under standby conditions.

This renders dynamic RAM unsuitable for battery-backed RAM applications. This is the type of RAM normally used for the main memory of computers, as it is much cheaper than static RAM. It is for this reason that battery-backed main RAM is never implemented. For the computer user it does not matter a great deal whether their machine is fitted with static RAM, dynamic RAM, or some of each. These terms are largely of academic interest except to the hardware designers.

ROM

You are likely to encounter a lot of references to RAM, and will probably come across almost as many references to ROM. This is again an acronym, and it is again a type of memory circuit. It stands for 'read only memory' and as this name suggests, the contents of ROM can only be *read* by the computer — there is no way of changing its contents. The program and (or) data stored in a ROM is placed there at the manufacturing stage, and can not be altered thereafter. This may not seem to be particularly useful, but the saving grace for ROM is that it is non-volatile. It is truly non-volatile, and does not need any batteries to maintain its contents when the main supply is switched off.

The main use of ROM is to store any programs or data that a computer will need at switch-on. For home computers this normally means a BASIC interpreter and the operating system. The BASIC interpreter is a programming language which you can use to write your own programs if you wish, or which you can just ignore if you are not interested in programming. The operating system is a program which provides some basic 'housekeeping' tasks. As a few examples, an operating system normally permits disks to be copied, programs to be run, data to be sent from a disk to a printer, and selected data to be copied from one disk to another. There must always be some form of operating system built into a computer so that it does not simply crash at switch-on.

Even if the main operating system is loaded from disk, there must always be some form of built-in operating system (or 'monitor program' as it is sometimes called) to load in the main operating system from disk. One of the more quaint computing terms is 'booting' or 'booting up', which is often used to describe the process of loading the operating system from disk. This is apparently derived from the fact that the operating system seems to be loading itself from the disk into the computer, which is rather like someone pulling themselves up by their bootstraps (straps rather than laces as it is an American term). Of course, the program is not loading itself at all, it is actually being loaded by the monitor program which is stored in ROM in the computer and automatically run each time it is switched on.

Another use for ROMs is as a means of storing applications programs. Some computers have internal sockets which can take ROMs containing applications programs, but it is more normal for this type of software to be sold as program cartridges. With these the ROM is on a small circuit board, possibly together with a small amount of additional circuitry, and it is contained in a small plastic case. The cartridge plugs into a socket on the exterior of the computer, usually on the top panel or at one side of the machine.

There are definite advantages to ROM software, the main one being that it is almost instantly available. Loading programs from disk and (especially) tape into RAM can be quite time consuming. ROM software could be loaded into RAM very quickly, but in most cases the program is run directly from the ROM so that there is no loading time whatever. Another advantage of ROM software is that it normally leaves the computer's RAM largely free for data supplied by the user. This is particularly useful in applications where the user will often input large amounts of data into the computer, which included sequencing and score writing.

Despite the advantages, ROM based software does not seem to have achieved great popularity. One obvious problem is that a lot of computers simply do not support ROM or cartridge based software. Where this facility is available, it tends to be relatively expensive. The raw material costs for a ROM or cartridge based software are substantially more than those of tape or disk based software. Where there is a choice between ROM/cartridge or disk based software I would be inclined to pay any extra cost for the ROM/ cartridge version, but in most cases there is no ROM or cartridge option.

EPROM

You may occasionally come across references to EPROMs. An EPROM is a kind of ROM chip, and EPROM stands for 'erasable programmable read only memory'. An EPROM differs from an ordinary ROM in that its contents can be changed, but only with the aid of a special EPROM programmer. It can not be written to in the same way as RAM. AN EPROM can also have its contents erased so that a new program can be written into it, but this can only be achieved using a special erasure unit (which shines ultra-violet light through a window in the top of the EPROM chip).

A lot of so-called ROM software is actually on EPROMs. The reason for this is that ROMs can only be produced in fairly large numbers as the cost is too high for short production runs. Producing true ROM software is probably only a practical proposition for fairly large companies who are confident of selling their products in large quantities. EPROMs, on the other hand, are practical even for one-off applications, and if necessary can always be reprogrammed. This is another example of something that is of purely academic importance to the user. Whether software is on ROM or EPROM, it should work just the same.

Megabytes and kilobytes

In computer specifications you will frequently encounter references to 'megabytes' and 'kilobytes'. We have already encountered the term byte, which is a number in the range 0 to 255. These numbers can be used singly to represent data and program instructions, but often two or more are used together for both program instructions and data. In practical applications large numbers of instructions and individual pieces of data tend to be used.

A kilobyte is one thousand bytes of data, or to be more precise it is 1024 bytes of data. This may seem a rather unusual number to choose, but if you multiply two by two, and keep multiplying the answer by two, you will eventually arrive at an answer of 1024. Computers operate in binary, which is a numbering system based on two and not ten as in the normal decimal numbering system. Hence numbers that are of significance in computing look to be of no consequence when expressed as decimal numbers.

A megabyte is roughly one million bytes, or to be more accurate, 1048576 bytes (i.e. 1024 × 1024 bytes). Both kilobytes and megabytes can be used to express the quantity of data, length of a program etc., but are also used when quantifying storage capacity of RAM, ROM, disk drives, etc. A 128k computer can therefore store over 128000 bytes of data and program instructions, which on the face of it is a vast amount of storage. On the other hand, you have to bear in mind that each program instruction might require two bytes, and will achieve very little. It takes a vast number of program instructions to perform complex tasks, and many music applications programs are very long. Also bear in mind that music applications can require large amounts of storage space for data. A MIDI sequencer will require 6 bytes of RAM for each note (three bytes for each note on message and three more for each note off message). Further bytes are required to provide timing information, say another two bytes per message. This means some ten bytes of storage are needed for each note, with further bytes being needed if there are additional MIDI messages such as pitch wheel types. Even with half of our 128k of memory set aside for data storage a multi-track sequence of moderate length could soon use it all up.

With an 8 byte computer you are unlikely to have more than 128k of memory available. In fact the popular 8 bit microprocessors are only able to handle a maximum of 64k of memory, and some hardware tricks are needed in order to provide the 128k of RAM which most 8 bit machines now seem to have as standard. Unfortunately, many programs for 8 bit computers equipped with expanded memory don't utilize it fully. In many cases the extra RAM is totally ignored.

The situation with 16 bit computers is very different, and these can usually have a megabyte or more of memory. Most programs that could usefully exploit these large quantities of RAM will normally do so. While 8 bit computers are far from obsolescent, little new music software seems to be produced for them. It is certainly true to say that the best and most powerful music software available runs on 16 bit machines, and usually requires something in the region of 500 kilobytes to 1 megabyte of RAM in order to run properly. For music applications a computer having a massive amount of memory is a definite advantage, and some would say it is essential.

Incidentally, kilobyte is often abbreviated to just K, and megabyte to M.

Getting it taped

For the long term storage of data the choice is normally between cassette tapes or computer disks. We will ignore here the non-standard forms of data storage which have appeared from time to time, but which have failed to achieve widespread use.

29

Cassette tapes certainly represent the cheapest method of storing data. Many households are already equipped with a suitable recorder, the cassettes themselves cost very little, and even with a system that stores data inefficiently, each one can hold large amounts of data. Cheapness is about the only advantage of cassettes for computer use though. Having used several computers with four or five cassette recorders (including three that were specifically designed for computer use), apart from one exception results were never totally reliable. In some cases it was difficult to recover stored data at all! The reliability problem is presumably solvable, but this still leaves cassettes with some distinct drawbacks. One of these is the slow rate at which data is saved onto tape and loaded back into the computer again. Some cassette systems are reasonably fast, but in general the faster the data transfer rate, the poorer the reliability of the system. One computer I owned had a cassette system that was reasonably reliable, but large games programs took about 15 minutes to load!

What is probably the greatest drawback of compact cassette data storage is that it can be difficult to track down the beginning of the program or data block that you wish to load into the computer. A common ploy is to use special computer cassettes which are very short. Using a large number of short cassette makes it relatively easy to track down and load the program or data you require, as there will probably only be two or three items on each side of the cassette. This method is still far from fast though, and having large numbers of cassettes is not very convenient either.

Disks

Disks and disk drives are a much more expensive solution to the problem, but a very much more satisfactory one. A lot of computers, including home computers, are now supplied complete with disk drives. These drives are often built into the computer. There seem to be several 8 bit computers which have cassette ports, but with 16 bit machines they are generally absent. There is then no option but to use a disk drive for long term data storage.

Disk storage is similar to ordinary tape recording in that it is a form of magnetic recording. The disk is made from a plastic material and it is coated with a magnetic oxide, very much like the coatings used on ordinary audio recording tapes. Data is recorded onto the disk in a series of concentric tracks. This is different from a conventional gramophone record which has the audio signal mechanically recorded onto a single spiralled groove on each side of the record. Each track is divided into a number of sectors. This general scheme of things is illustrated in Figure 2.1, but in practice there would be many more tracks and sectors than shown in this diagram.

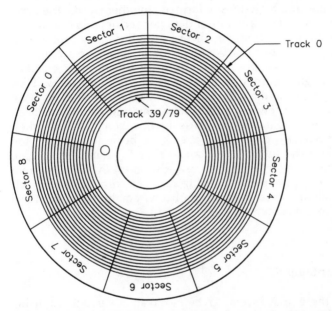

Figure 2.1 Data is organised on a disk using a system of tracks and sectors

The number of tracks and sectors depends on the particular disk format used, but normally there are either 40 or 80 tracks per side of the disk, and about 8 or 9 sectors. Some disk drives use both sides of the disk while other use only one side. In most cases drives that use both sides of a disk have two recording/playback heads, one for each side of the disk. Consequently, there is no need to use one side of the disk and then turn it over in order to use the second side. The disk will only work if it is fitted the right way up, and in the majority of cases the user does not know which side of the disk is being used. This is up to the computer, and it may even store part of a program (or whatever) on one side of the disk and the rest of it on the other. With modern computers tending to deal in large amounts of data, and some disk drives have relatively small storage capacities, it certainly makes sense in a lot of cases to lump both sides of the disk together in this fashion. Note that some computers that use 3 inch disks (the Amstrad CPC6128 for instance) do have double sided disks which must be turned over in order to use the second side.

Further complicating the subject of disk formats, there are single, double, and high density formats. In other words, the drive can place the standard amount of data per sector, squeeze double that amount onto each sector, or use a high density format that uses more sectors per track with a lot of data per sector. Yet another complication arises in the form of several different disk sizes. The original computer disks were the 8 inch variety. Disk sizes are merely the diameter of the disk. The 8 inch disks have not been used on new computers for some time, and have been usurped by the 5.25 inch type. These are now being challenged by 3 inch and 3.5 inch disks. The latter have been accepted by the computer industry as the new standard, and presumably in time the other disk sizes will fall from use. However, in the mean time a lot of new computers are still being supplied with 5.25 and 3 inch disks, and all four disk sizes will probably remain in common use for some time to come.

Disk advantages

Although there may seem to be no real advantage in using magnetic disk recording instead of tape recording, for computer use a disk system is vastly superior. One reason for this is that a disk system is specifically designed for storing and retrieving computer data, and very high levels of reliability are achieved together with high rates of data transfer. Loading times are typically less than a tenth of those provided by a fast cassette interface. The main advantage is the speed with which the beginning of a program or block of data can be located. It often takes less than a second for the required section of the disk to be located and the transfer of data to commence. The important point here is that it is not necessary to go through the disk track-by-track, and sector by sector, until the required data is located. The disk drive can jump almost instantly to any desired track and sector.

Of course, this random access capability only brings speed advantages if the disk drive knows on which sector and track each program or block of data commences. In practice a fairly sophisticated method of control is used, which makes use of an operating system program in the computer, some sophisticated hardware to control the disk, and information stored on the disk. Before a disk can be used it must be formatted. This is achieved using a program supplied with the computer or the disk drive. In many cases the format program is part of the computer's operating system. One function of the format program is to put marker signals onto the the disk which indicate the positions of the tracks and sectors. It also sets aside some tracks and sectors to act as a 'directory', which shows what 'files' are on the disk, and where they are located.

Some directory systems are quite sophisticated, and do not insist on files being on contiguous tracks/sectors of the disk. If a number of files are recorded onto the disk and then some of them are erased, this can leave the disk with a lot of small areas which are unused. With the less sophisticated disk systems, if the control program can not find a single unused block on the disk which is large enough to take the file you wish to save to disk, it will report that it is unable to save the file to disk. The better disk control systems will always save a file on disk if there is sufficient disk space, even if the file has to be fragmented into dozens of small blocks of data. The directory tells the control program where to find each block of data for the required file. This aids efficient use of disks, but there is a slight disadvantage in that having to jump around all over the place in order to read a file is inevitably a bit slower than having the file read from one continuous block on the disk.

Disk capacity

Just how much data can be stored on a disk depends on the disk size and the format used. You need to be careful when comparing disk storage capacities as some computer manufacturers quote the basic (unformatted) capacity of the disk, while others quote the capacity that remains after the formatting process. The difference is usually quite substantial, with around 15% to 30% of a disk's capacity usually being given over to formatting information. The table shown below gives the approximate formatted and unformatted capacities for a range of 5.25 inch disc formats.

These disk capacities can only be approximations because not all drives/computers format the disks in exactly the same way. They are a good guide to the amount of storage that can be expected

Disk format	Basic	Formatted
Single sided single density 40 track	125 k	100 k
Double sided single density 40 track	250 k	180 k
Single sided double density 40 track	250 k	180 k
Double sided double density 40 track	500 k	360 k
Single sided single density 80 track	250 k	180 k
Double sided single density 80 track	500 k	360 k
Single sided double density 80 track	500 k	360 k
Double sided double density 80 track	1 M	720 k
High density	1.6 M	1.2 M

from a given type of disk. It is worth mentioning that these are the possible disk formats, but some of them are little used in practice. Also, not all 5.25 disk systems conform to one of these standards, although most recent computers seem to use one or other of these. Basically the same formats are used for 3.5 inch disks, but in the case of high density disks there is a formatted capacity of 1.44 megabytes per disk. 3 inch disks normally have 40 tracks with 90k of formatted capacity per side, or twice as many tracks with double the capacity.

Obtaining the right disks should not be difficult because the manual for the computer or disk drive should clearly state the type that is required. In general, there is no problem if you use a disk that has a higher specification than the drive requires. A double sided disk can be utilized where a single sided type is required, or a double density disk can be used where a single density disk is required. This is likely to be more expensive than obtaining the right disks, but would presumably be a worthwhile ploy in the event of supply difficulties.

As a point of interest, all disks seem to have the magnetic coating on both sides, and it is rumoured that single sided disks have never been manufactured! The difference between single and double sided disks is that the double sided variety is guaranteed to give satisfactory results on both sides of the disk, while the single sided type are only guaranteed to have one side fully operational. You might be able to get away with using single sided disks in a double sided drive, but the saving in cost would hardly seem to merit the risk of losing valuable data. The same is probably also true for some bargain disks, although I have never had any problems with low cost disks obtained from reputable suppliers.

I would not recommend using high density disks in anything other than a high density disk drive. I once got some high density disks and some 40 track double density double sided disks swapped over. My mistake came to light because, surprisingly, the 40 track disks formatted perfectly as high density 1.2 megabyte types, but the high density disks would not format reliably as 360k double density types. It would seem that others who have tried to use high density disks as double or single density types have found the same problem. The magnetic coating on high density disks seems to be a special formulation that ordinary drives can not always handle satisfactorily. This is presumably rather like using a metal or chrome dioxide audio cassette in a cheap recorder that is not equipped to handle them. Results are often worse than those obtained from cheap cassettes which the recorder can handle properly.

In the flesh

So much for the theoretical side of computer disks — what do they look like in practice and how do you obtain trouble-free operation from them? The 5.25 inch disks have the appearance shown in Figure 2.2. An important point to realise is that computer disks

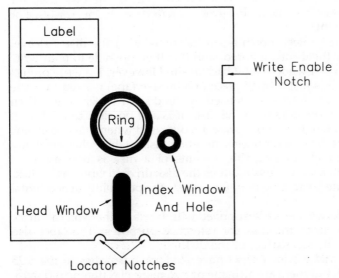

Figure 2.2 The make-up of a 5.25 inch floppy disk

should never be removed from their protective sleeve. They are placed into the computer still within this sealed sleeve, and the sleeve locks into place inside the drive machine. With 5.25 inch drives there is a locking lever on the drive which must be pushed to the down position before the disk is accessed, and this securely locks the disk in place. Returning this lever to the up position ejects the disk. Computer disks are sometimes called 'floppy' disks, because the actual disk part is made from a thin and literally very floppy material. In the case of 5.25 inch disks they are also floppy in the sense that the sleeve is often far from rigid. Some disks are better than others in this respect. However, you always need to take care not to buckle these disks when inserting them into the drive.

The drive heads are able to reach the disk via 'windows' cut into the sleeve. A hub ring at the middle of the disk reinforces it and aids long working life (this ring is absent on some of the cheaper disks, and for some reason is not included on many high density types). There is a hole in the sleeve close to the hub ring, and if you rotate a disk within its sleeve you will find a matching hole in the disk itself. This operates in conjunction with a photocell circuit in the disk drive, and it helps the disk control system to navigate its way around the disk by providing a known reference point. Note that this hole is inside the part of the disk used for data storage so that it does not interfere with the track/sector arrangement.

A 'write protect' notch is cut in one edge of the disk's sleeve. Normally this is just ignored, and it is then possible to both write data onto a disk and read it back again. However, if a write protect tab (which is just a small piece of adhesive tape) is fixed over the write protect notch, it is sensed by the disk drive which will then refuse to write data onto the disk. It is still possible to read from the disk though. A write protect tab is used when a disk contains important data, or for master program disks, where the possibility of accidentally erasing the contents of a disk is best avoided. Erasing data from a disk requires the disk drive to write to the disk, and a write protect tag therefore avoids the possibility of accidental erasure.

All disks are normally supplied with labels so that you can mark the contents of the disk for reference purposes. The label also indicates the top surface of the disk.

3 inch and 3.5 inch disks have obvious similarities to the 5.25 inch type, but there are also one or two marked differences (Figure 2.3). The most noticeable of these is that they are much thicker and

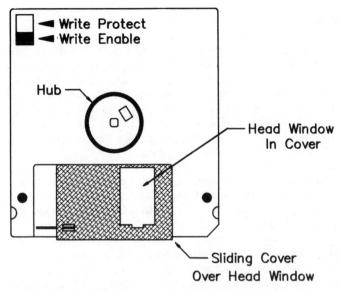

Figure 2.3 A 3.5 inch disk is more refined than the 5.25 inch type. In particular there is a spring loaded sliding cover over the head window

are contained in a rigid plastic case. Although these disks are smaller, the greater thickness means that they require a comparable amount of storage space to the 5.25 inch type. They are much less vulnerable to physical damage though, and are preferred to the 5.25 inch disks by many users. 3 inch and 3.5 inch disks lock into the drive without the aid of a locking lever. There is a push button which is used to eject the disk from the drive.

Another difference is that the windows for the recording heads are covered over by metal 'curtains' which slide out of the way when the disk is placed into the drive. This leaves the disk totally enclosed and much less vulnerable to physical damage. This is important as a lot of data is being crammed onto quite a small disk, and any dust or other contamination on the disk's surface is more likely to cause problems than it is with the larger 5.25 inch disks.

A third difference is that the two smaller disk sizes do not have the stick-on write protect tabs. Instead, there is a little plastic slider which can be set to enable or disable writing to the disk, as required. The 3 inch disks have two of the sliders, one for each side of the disk.

Do's and dont's

Unless you are unlucky, properly used and handled disks should provide years of trouble-free operation. Having used numerous disks of various types over many years, the only major problems I have encountered have been due to my own carelessness or equipment failures, rather than to any disk faults. If you do not treat computer disks with due respect then you can reasonably expect to have frequent problems and masses of lost data. Here are some do's and dont's of disk handling.

1 With the 5.25 inch disks do not handle the disk itself through the head windows. Greasy finger prints can attract dust onto the surface of the disk, and could even attack and damage the magnetic coating of the disk. With 3.5 and 3 inch disks, resist the temptation to pull back the metal shutters and look at the disk. Dust can get in when the shutters are open, and you could easily scratch the surface of the disk with a fingernail.

2 Keep 5.25 inch disks in their paper envelopes when they are not in use, and preferably store them in a proper disk storage box. Proper storage boxes are less important for 3 inch and 3.5 inch disks, particularly the 3 inch type which are often supplied complete with individual library boxes. Some form of well organised storage is still preferable thought.

3 Keep all computer disks well away from any powerful magnets. Magnets are to be found in a number of electrical and electronic gadgets, including virtually anything that contains a small electric motor or a loudspeaker. Telephones are also supposed to be capable of erasing data from disks if the disks are kept very close to them for a few days.

4 Always insert disks into a drive very carefully, especially the 5.25 inch type. Make sure you get the disk the right way round and the right way up.

5 Disks should not be subjected to extreme temperatures. Most manufacturers seem to recommend that they should be kept between 10 and 52 degrees Centigrade.

6 Probably most disks that are rendered useless are damaged by something like someone spilling coffee on them, sitting or treading on them, etc. Do not leave disks where they are vulnerable to careless damage of this type. If a disk should become buckled it might be possible to flatten it out and recover some of the data on it, but some data loss is almost certain to occur. Similarly, it might be possible to clean off a dirty disc, but the chances are that you will suffer some data loss. Do not put a contaminated disk into a

disk drive until the disk has been properly and very thoroughly cleaned off. Other wise you are likely to spread the contamination to the drives heads and from there to other disks.

7   When writing on disk labels, use a fibre-tip pen not a ball-point type, and only press gently. Position disk labels at one corner of the disk sleeve so that, as far as possible, it is over an empty part of the sleeve. Writing hard using something like a ball-point pen or a hard grade pencil could easily damage the disk, or with 3 inch and 3.5 inch disks there is a slight risk of damaging the rigid sleeve. Believe it or not, there are special disk label pens. If you press too hard the fibre-tip of the pen snaps off so that damage to disks is avoided!

Hard disks

A hard disk drive (also known as a'fixed' or 'Winchester' disk) works in essentially the same way as an ordinary disk drive, but is a highly refined form of drive. Hard drives differ from ordinary disk drives in two very important respects. The most obvious of these is that the disk is literally 'fixed' in the drive, and can not be removed. The disk is normally contained in a sealed case which keeps out dust and dirt, which would have even more disastrous consequences than with a floppy disk. The disk is generally not a single disk, but two or four (possibly more) mounted one above the other on a common spindle. This helps to give hard disks their very high storage capacities. The minimum storage capacity is about 10 megabytes, while 20 to 40 megabyte drives are now commonplace. Some drives have a capacity well in excess of 100 megabytes. Of course, with the disk not being interchangeable it is important that it has a very large capacity. It must be capable of storing all the applications programs you wish to run, with sufficient spare capacity for all the data you generate and wish to store on the hard disk.

The other main difference between floppy and hard disks is that hard disks rotate all the time, and not just when you actually access them. While the high storage capacity of hard disks is a definite advantage, probably their most important advantage is the speed at which data can be written to and read back from them. Also, the recording/playback heads can be very rapidly moved to any desired track and sector of the disk. Getting data to and from a hard disk is not quite as quick as getting data direct from RAM, but good hard disk systems certain give RAM a run for its money.

It is quite common for complex programs to use part of a hard disk as a sort of pseudo RAM when the computer has insufficient RAM. Obviously there is no point in having the ability to move the heads almost instantly to any desired part of the disk if it then takes several seconds for the disk to start and get up to operating speed. Having the disk rotating continuously avoids this problem. The disk rotates much faster than a floppy disk, with speeds usually being a few thousand rpm as opposed to the few hundred rpm of a floppy disk. The high rotation speed enables data to be loaded and retrieved much faster than can be achieved with conventional floppy disk systems. About ten or more times faster in fact. The speed of data transfer may well be limited by the computer rather than by the hard disk system.

Sub-directories

While the large capacity of a hard disk has its advantages, it also brings its problems. With data stored on a large number of floppy disks, things are compartmentalised, and it is not too difficult to track down any desired piece of data provided you are reasonably logical about the way the disks are organised. With megabytes of data all on one disk, finding the required data file could be difficult. Data is stored in named files, and if you should happen to forget the name of a file you might have to look through a list of hundreds of file names in order to track down the one you want.

To make things more manageable most data and programs are stored in sub-directories. In effect, the disk is divided into a number of compartments, with the usual arrangement being to have each program and its data in one of these 'sub-directories', as these compartments are called. If required, each sub-directory can have further sub-directories. For example, data produced by a program could be stored in the form of a separate sub-directory for each month. This would make it easier to locate a piece of data produce some months earlier provided you have some idea when it was generated. If necessary, it is normally possible to produce sub-directories of sub-directories indefinitely, but obviously things could easily become less manageable rather than more convenient if things are allowed to get out of hand.

A convenient way of viewing sub-director structures is to draw up a directory tree, as in the example of Figure 2.4. The main directory from which the initial sub-directories branch out is called the 'root' directory incidentally. Some operating systems allow the use of sub-directories with floppy disks, but except with the higher

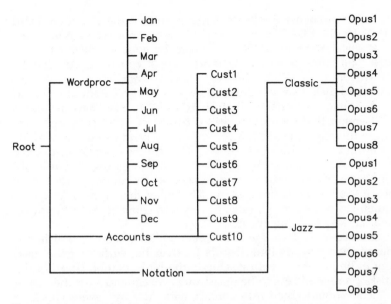

Figure 2.4 An example of a directory tree. Note that it is possible to have files of the same name provided they are in separate sub-directories

capacity types, there is often no point in bothering to use them. It is worth pointing out that sub-directories are not physical partitions on a disk. Files in various sub-directories are liberally scattered across the disk and mixed in together. The sub-directories only exist in the form of additional information in the directory on the disk, so that the operating system can filter out all but the files designated as being in the particular sub-directory you are interested in.

Getting your back-up

Hard disks clearly have definite advantages, and some complex programs will run well only on a computer that is equipped with one. There are even a few programs that will only operate on computers equipped with a hard disk. They do have a few disadvantages though. One of these is their relatively high cost. Apart from hard disks for the IBM PCs and compatibles they tend to be very expensive, often costing more than the computer! Hard disks for the IBM PCs and compatibles sell in such large numbers that costs are relatively low, but a really good 40 megabyte hard disk still costs substantially more than a cheap PC compatible. However, if you will be running software that really merits the use of a hard disk it should prove to be well worth the additional cost.

A common complaint about hard disks is that they are noisy. Remember that the disk rotates continuously at high speed. The drive therefore produces a continuous whirring sound the whole time that the computer is in use. This can be a bit of a nuisance when running programs such as word processors, but it could obviously be very distracting indeed when running music software. Some hard disks are much better than others as far as quietness is concerned, but I have yet to come across a hard disk that is close to being silent.

A hard disk is a piece of precision engineering which has aerodynamic heads that literally fly over the surface of the disk, not quite in contact with it. Due to the high rotation speed of the disk, there are likely to be disastrous consequences for the disk if a head should come into contact with it. Any severe shock or vibration is likely to damage a hard disk, and they must be treated very carefully.

What makes matters worse is that the process of repairing a hard disk often results in all or most of the software and data it contains being lost! To guard against this it is standard practice to periodically back up (copy) all the data on a hard disk to floppy disks, or some other back-up medium. Apart from these periodic back-ups, it is also normal to put onto floppy disks copies of any files that you generate, as you generate them, or to do frequent back-ups using a system that only backs up newly produced or changed files. In the event of a hard disk failure it is then a relatively painless process to restore the repaired disk to its former state.

Backing up a hard disk to floppy disks is a rather tedious process. It can take a few hours to complete a back up of an average sized disk. A quicker method is to use a tape streamer, which is a device designed specifically for back-up purposes. It uses tape cartridges with continuous loops of tape, and will produce a back-up somewhat faster than using floppy disks. The cartridges have a capacity which is comparable to that of a hard disk, and frequent changing of the cartridges is unnecessary. In many cases one cartridge will hold a complete back-up of the disk. The only real disadvantage of a tape streamer is that it is quite expensive, and most users seem to settle for occasional tedium of backing-up onto floppy disks.

Figure 2.5 The Amiga 1500 has twin floppy disk drives (see Chapter 4 for more info on the Amiga computers)

3 Ports and peripherals

If you were to obtain the most powerful computer around, complete with mouse, high quality keyboard, and high resolution colour monitor, the chances are that it would be virtually useless unless it was augmented by some peripheral devices. How would you get hard copy of documents, scores, or whatever, without some form of printer or a plotter? Add-on units such as these would only be usable with the computer if there was somewhere to plug them in. In this chapter we will consider popular computer peripherals, and the computer ports that are needed in order to couple them to a computer.

A common complaint in the early days of home computers concerned the plethora of non-standard interfaces. A lot of the computers produced back then were equipped with ports, particularly printer ports, that permitted only the computer manufacturer's own peripherals to be used with their machines. This had an obvious attraction for computer manufacturers, since having bought one of their computers you then had to buy a lot of additional products from them if you wanted to expand the system. It was not popular with the customers because they had only a very limited choice of add-on products that could be used with their computers. Furthermore, the products they had to choose from were not necessarily particularly good, innovative, or cheap. A lot of third-party interfaces were produced to enable some of these non-standards ports to be connected to peripherals that did have standard interfaces.

Although manufacturers' own interfaces are not totally unknown in modern computing, they are certainly much more rare. With virtually all the current popular computers there are one or two standard ports for use with a seemingly unending choice of printers, plotters, modems, etc. Consequently, in this chapter we will not be dealing in any depth with non-standard interfaces.

Parallel lines

Probably the most common type of computer interface is the parallel printer type, and a printer is almost certainly the most popular computer peripheral. Parallel printer ports are also known as 'Centronics' ports, presumably as this port was originated by the company of the same name. A parallel port is one where data is carried over a number of connecting wires and a earth line. In the case of a Centronics type printer port there are eight data lines (D0 to D7) plus an earth wire. The signal on each wire is either at a very low potential (about 0 to 2 volts), or a slightly higher potential of about 3 to 5 volts. These levels are respectively called 'logic 0' and 'logic 1', or just 'low' and 'high'. With eight data connections and two states for each one, there are some 256 different combinations of logic states that can be produced on these lines. These are numbered from 0 (all lines low) to 255 (all lines high). In others words, the eight data lines enable data to be transferred one byte at a time.

Figure 3.1 shows connection details for the standard 36 way connector used for parallel printer ports at the printer end of the

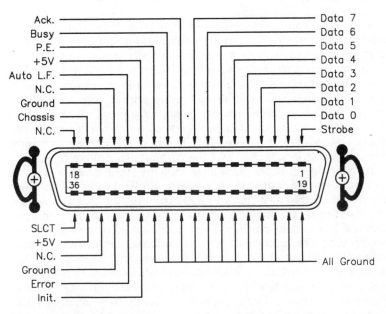

Figure 3.1 Centronics (parallel) port connection details

system. There is no true standard at the computer end of the link, where a variety of connector types are in common use. You need to buy a printer lead specifically for your make and model of computer, and with few exceptions, no other type will be suitable.

From Figure 3.1 it will be apparent that there are a number of lines apart from the data ones and an earth connection. There are actually a number of earth leads. Only one of these is needed in order to provide the earth connection between the computer and the printer. The additional ones are mainly included to act as screens between the data lines. A common problem with parallel interfaces is that of signals on one data line tending to be coupled into an adjacent data line. This can give severely scrambled data even with quite short connecting cables. Having an earth lead between each data lead minimizes this problem, but the maximum recommended length for parallel printer leads is still only two metres (but a good quality 3 metre cable should give reliable results).

Handshaking

Some of the connecting wires are used for such things as the printer indicating to the computer that it is out of paper, but these lines are not always implemented, particularly at the computer end of the system. The handshake lines (strobe, busy, and acknowledge) are not in this category, and at least the strobe line and one of the other two lines will always be present at both ends of the system. In fact all three lines are normally present on printers.

In order to understand the concept of handshaking you need to understand why it is necessary. The first problem with an eight line plus earth interface is that the computer can place a series of eight bit codes onto the data lines, but the printer has no way of knowing when a new code is present. It could monitor the lines and assumed that any change in the code means that a new byte of data is present, but what if the computer sends two or three identical bytes in succession. The printer would interpret this as a single byte. In order to get around this problem an extra connection is needed, and this is the strobe line. Normally this line is high, but each time a fresh byte of data is placed on the data lines, the strobe is briefly pulsed low. This makes it quite clear to the printer that new data is present and ready to be acted on, thus avoiding either missed bytes or bytes being read twice.

This still leaves a second problem in that a computer can place data onto the parallel connecting lines far faster than any printer can print out the data. The maximum rate at which data can be sent over a parallel interface depends on the particular electronics used in both the computer and the printer, but a rate of 500000 bytes per second is well within the bounds of reason. A fast printer could manage perhaps 200 to 300 bytes per second. In order to prevent the computer from sending data at a rate which is too fast for the printer to keep up with, a further handshake line is needed. This enables the printer to indicate to the computer that data transmission should be stopped until further notice, so that overloading and loss of data are avoided. This is the purpose of the 'acknowledge' and 'busy' lines.

The acknowledge line is normally high and it stays high when a byte of data is received. It is pulsed low by the printer when it has processed a byte of data and is ready to receive the next one. The busy line is normally in the low state, but it is set high by the printer when a byte of data is received. It is returned to the low state when the byte of data has been processed and the printer is ready to receive the next one.

Serial data

Parallel ports are used for printers, and sometimes for plotters, but are little used for anything else. There is a more general form of computer interface in the form of the RS232C serial type. This is sometimes used for printers, and is often used for plotters, modems, mice and a wide range of specialized computer peripherals. Some computers (such as the BBC series) have a similar serial interface − the RS423 type. This is largely compatible with the RS232C type and can be used with peripherals that are intended for operation with an RS232C port.

A serial port differs from a parallel type in that it has only one data line. This is used to carry all eight bits of data, which obviously can not be sent simultaneously. Instead, they are sent one at a time, in sequence, starting with D0 and working through to D7. Parallel ports operate with standard 0 to 5 volt logic levels, but in order to give the system greater range, the RS232C interface operates with signal levels of approximately plus and minus 12 volts. Do not be tempted to connect an RS232C port to one which uses standard logic levels − the RS232C port is unlikely to be affected but the other port is quite likely to be damaged.

Serial interfaces can be either synchronous or asynchronous. A synchronous type requires a minimum of three connecting wires; the earth line, a data line, and a clock line. The clock line is used to tell the receiving equipment when to read the data line. Synchronous serial links are relatively rare, and the RS232C system is not normally implemented in this form. Instead, it is used to provide asynchronous communications, where a minimum of just the earth line and the data line are required. The data line is used to tell the receiving equipment when a new byte is being sent and it is time to start reading in the bits of data.

This operates in a very simple manner where the data line is held at a standby state until a byte of data must be sent. It is then switched to the other level for a certain period of time, which indicates to the receiving equipment that data is about to be placed on the data line. This initial signal is called the 'start bit'. The transmitting hardware then places the eight bits of data onto the data line, one by one. The receiving device checks the data line at regular intervals so that it can read in the state of each bit, and put together a full byte of data. Finally, the data line is returned to the standby level for a period of time that is equal to the duration of the start bit, or double this duration. This is the 'stop bit' or bits, and it merely ensures that there is a suitable gap between bytes so that the receiving equipment can easily sort out one byte from another.

Baud rates

The start bit provides only a very crude form of synchronization, and one that is inadequate on its own. For an asynchronous communications system to operate properly it is essential that the rate at which bits are sent out from the transmitter is accurately matched to the rate at which the receiving hardware reads them in. This is achieved by having a series of fixed transmission/reception rates, or 'baud' rates as they are known. These baud rates are 50, 75, 110, 150, 300, 600, 1200, 1800, 2400, 4800, 9600, and 19200 baud. These figures represent the number of bits sent per second with continuous transmission. They do not represent a particularly fast rate of transfer, bearing in mind that about ten bits are required per byte. A rate of 1200 baud for example, represents a maximum transmission rate of only about 120 bytes per second. However, the rates of transfer are perfectly adequate for many applications. Unlike parallel interfaces, serial interfaces will operate with long cables. Even at the higher baud rates an RS232C interface can be used with connecting cables many metres long.

Complications

An RS232C port is certainly a very useful form of interface to have on a computer, but RS232C links have a reputation for giving problems in practice. Unfortunately, this reputation is probably well deserved! One problem is simply the sheer number of permutations that are possible with this system. A great deal of care needs to be taken when setting up RS232C equipment in order to ensure that the type of serial signal being transmitted is the one that the receiving equipment expects to receive. As we have already seen, there are a number of standard baud rates. There are further complications though. One of these is the word format.

All RS232C asynchronous signals start with one start bit, but there can be five, six, seven or eight data bits, and one or two stop bits. In computing applications normally only seven or eight data bits are used, which slightly simplifies matters.

There is a further complication though, in the form of parity error checking. This is a very simple form of error checking which relies on always having an even number of logic 1s in each byte (even parity) or an odd number of logic 1s (odd parity). Obviously neither odd or even parity occur naturally, and the transmitting hardware has to add an extra bit to some bytes in order to maintain odd or even parity, as required. These extra bits are added between the last data bit and the first stop bit. In practice parity checking seems to be little used. It is far from 100% reliable as a double glitch could alter two bits, leaving the parity intact but the byte corrupted. The waveform diagram of Figure 3.2 might help to clarify the way in which serial data is coded onto a single data line.

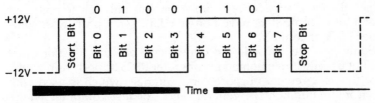

Figure 3.2 An example RS232C serial waveform. In this case there is no parity bit

With a number of standard baud rates, odd, even, or no parity, seven, or eight data bits, and one or two stop bits, the number of possible baud rate and word format permutations is substantial. I suppose that it does not matter too much if you do not fully understand all about baud rates and word formats. The important thing is to ensure that the transmitting and receiving units are set to the same baud rates and word formats. You are unlikely to get a satisfactory data transfer if they are in any way set up differently. The settings used may not be too important, but it is probably not worth bothering with parity checking. The baud rate should be high enough to keep up with the rate at which the peripheral device can perform, where this is feasible. One stop bit is better than two in that it takes less time and aids rapid data exchange. The use of eight data bits is safer than using seven bits. Some data only requires seven bits (including text which conforms to the normal ASCII standard of coding), but sometimes the full eight bits are needed. Where it is supported by both pieces of equipment, 9600 baud operation with no parity, eight data bits, and one stop bit is a safe and popular choice.

Bidirectional communication

An important difference between a Centronics type parallel interface and an RS232C serial type is that the parallel variety provides communications in only one direction. By having two parallel interfaces, one for transmission and one for reception, it would actually be possible to have two way communications. In practice computers only seem to use a Centronics style interface as a means of sending data to a printer, plotter, or similar peripheral. A computer RS232C interface is invariably a two way type. It can, for example, provide two way communication between two computers.

Figure 3.3 shows connection details for a standard RS232C port, which uses a 25 way D type connector. It is only fair to point out that a lot of computers have non-standard serial ports with some other form of connector.

Some pins are unused, and others have obscure functions that are not usually implemented in computer RS232C ports (remember that this is a general purpose serial interface which is used with electronic equipment in general, and not just computer equipment). For the most basic of two way links you only need connect

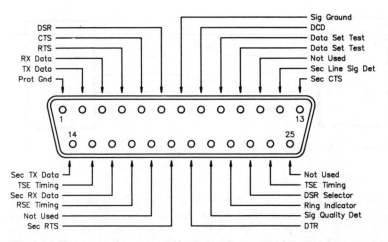

Figure 3.3 The connections to an RS232C (serial) port. Not all computers use this type of connector

the two ground (earth) terminals of the two interfaces, and cross-couple the data input and data output terminals.

More handshaking

In common with a Centronics style parallel interface, an RS232C type can have handshaking. The handshake lines are not always needed because in some applications the flow of data will be at a fairly modest rate, and there will be no risk of the receiving device becoming overloaded. The handshaking operates in a very simple manner, with the basic arrangement being to have a handshake output on the receiving device coupled to a handshake input on the transmitting device. The handshake output goes to one logic level to indicate that the receiving device is ready to receive data, or the alternative logic level in order to request a hold-off. For a two way interface, separate handshaking is used for each data line. A basic five line (two way with handshaking link) is shown in Figure 3.4.

In practice matters are complicated by the fact there are two types of RS232C device, known as 'data terminal equipment' (DTE) and 'data communications equipment' (DCE). In computing

51

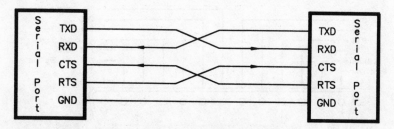

Figure 3.4 The standard 5 wire RS232C interconnections

virtually all RS232C ports are of the DTE variety, which means that they send out data on their output line and receive it on their input line. DCE equipment, somewhat strangely, receives data on its output and transmits it on its input terminal. The handshake lines also operate in the same topsy-turvy manner. This may seem to be a bit ludicrous, but the idea is that in a normal RS232C system there should be one DTE device and one DCE type. The connecting cable is then very simple, with a 25 way D connector at each end, and with each terminal of one D connector coupled through to the same pin on the other one. Note that the only difference between DTE and DCE ports is their method of connection to the 25 way D connector. In other respects they are the same, and a simple adaptor can convert a piece of equipment from DCE to DTE operation (or vice versa).

Apart from one or two computers (such as the Sinclair QL) which have two serial ports, with one configured as a DTE type and the other connected for DCE operation, computer equipment has ports configured for DTE operation. This means that a cable of the type described above will not give satisfactory results, as it will connect inputs to inputs and outputs to outputs. RS232C ports have current limiting on their outputs so that this should not cause any damage, but obviously it will not give a data transfer. What is required is a cable that has cross coupling so that inputs connect to outputs. A cable of this type is known as a 'null modem' cable, and a typical method of connection is shown in Figure 3.5.

Having made up more computer connecting cables than I care to remember over the last ten years, my advice is to avoid making up your own RS232C cables, even if you are quite deft with a soldering iron! Matters might seem to be quite straightforward, but in practice there are plenty of things that can go wrong. The hardware may not be quite as 'standard' as it is supposed to be.

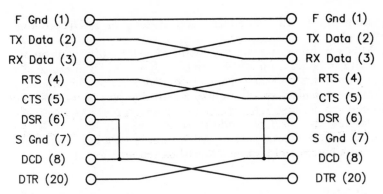

Figure 3.5 The interconnections used in most null modem RS232C leads

In particular, there are numerous computers and peripherals which use a connector other than the 25 way D type. Where a ready-made, tried and tested cable is available, it will probably not cost much more than the raw materials, and it could save a lot of wasted time.

MIDI expansion

As I stated at the beginning of this chapter, we are mainly concerned with standard computer ports. On the other hand, we can not totally ignore computer specific ports. Presumably most people who are interested in setting up a computer based music system will wish to control MIDI instruments from their computer. In order to do this the computer must be fitted with a MIDI interface. Unfortunately, as yet MIDI interfaces are not included as part of standard specification on most computers. At the time of writing this, the only really popular computers that have built-in MIDI interfaces are the Atari ST series. Understandably, these have become especially popular amongst the electronic music fraternity.

The fact that a computer does not have a built-in MIDI interface does not mean that it is not suitable for use as the controller in a MIDI system. For all the current and popular microcomputers there seem to be at least a few add-on MIDI interfaces available, plus at least a sprinkling of MIDI software. In some cases there are a number of MIDI interfaces and dozens of MIDI programs available.

Most computers are equipped with some form of expansion port which can be used for add-on units such as a MIDI interface. The exact form this port takes varies from computer to computer, and it might be called something like a cartridge port, a user port, or some form of 'bus', rather than an expansion port. As a couple of examples, for the Commodore 64/128 series it is normally the cartridge port that is used for MIDI interfaces, while for the BBC series of computers it is the 1MHz bus that is normally utilized.

Card tricks

In most cases an add-on MIDI port takes the form of a small plastic box which plugs onto the appropriate port at the rear of the computer. In a few cases the box is attached to multi-way lead and connector which plugs into the rear or underside of the computer. A few computers have a very different approach to expansion, and use internally fitted expansion cards. The most popular computer which uses this method of expansion is the IBM PC series and the countless IBM compatible machines.

A MIDI interface for a machine of this type consists of a printed circuit board with the MIDI sockets fitted at one end. The printed circuit board slots into a connector on the computer's main circuit board, or 'motherboard' as it is termed. A blanking plate is removed from the rear of the computer, and the sockets on the board fit into the space formerly occupied by this plate. A bolt fixes the board firmly in place by securing it to the case of the computer. With the computer's outer casing replaced, the MIDI port appears to be built-in rather than an add-on.

This is a very neat solution to the problem, but it is only fair to point out that most computers which permit internal expansion of this type are pretty huge. You would probably need a large and strong desk in order to accommodate one properly and safely. Floor standing 'tower' cases are now becoming quite popular for computers of this type.

In a few cases the normal method of adding a MIDI port is other than fitting it to any form of expansion port or bus. The Amiga series of computers are probably the only really popular computers where an alternative approach to the problem has been adopted. The standard method with the Amiga is to have a simple piece of electronics fitted onto its RS232C serial port. This works well because MIDI uses a form of asynchronous serial signal, very much like that of an RS232C interface. In fact the word format used is the popular RS232C one of one start bit, eight data bits, one stop bit, and no parity.

In isolation

The signal levels are totally different though. Whereas an RS232C signal uses positive and negative voltages, a MIDI interface operates by switching a small electric current on and off. It is a bit like switching a light bulb on and off, but the current is only a small fraction of that consumed by a small torch bulb (just 5 milliamps to be precise). It is actually a light emitting diode (LED) that is being switched on and off, and this forms part of a component called an 'opto-isolator'. The light output of the LED is directed at a photo-sensitive electronic component, and both components are contained in an opaque case so that ambient light does not reach the photocell. When the LED switches on, it in turn switches on the photocell, and the signal is coupled through the device.

This may seem like a clever but grossly overcomplicated means of handling things, but it does bring its advantages. The whole point of an opto-isolator is that it couples a signal from one circuit to another, but there is no direct electrical connection between the two circuits. Remember that the coupling between the input and output of the opto-isolator is a light beam, not wires. This electrical isolation avoids the possibly disastrous consequences of connecting together various computers, musical instruments, and possibly other devices such as MIDI controlled mixers and effects units. Provided everything in the system is earthed to the mains earth lead there is no problem. However, much modern electronics uses double insulation to provide safety, with no connection being made to the mains earth lead. This can result in substantial voltage difference between the earths of two pieces of mains powered equipment, and the likelihood of one or both of them becoming damaged if they are connected together. This is a very real danger, as I once learned the hard way.

The opto-isolation at MIDI inputs is guaranteed to withstand a minimum of about 2500 volts, which is more than adequate to remove the danger of equipment being damaged due to these voltage differences. The isolation brings other advantages, one of which is reduced risk of the dreaded 'hum' or 'earth' loops. These are probably all too familiar to users of electronic music equipment, and audio equipment in general. The opto-isolation does not guarantee that problems with 'hum' due to earth loops will be avoided, but it does eliminate one possible cause of them. Another advantage of opto-isolation is that it discourages stray coupling of electronic noise from a computer to the audio circuits of instruments in the system. Computers produce electrical noise in prolific amounts, and this could easily produce unwanted buzzing sounds on the audio output of a music system if it was not comprehensively blocked.

Returning to the Amiga computers and their RS232C MIDI interfaces, providing opto-isolation at an RS232C input requires only some very simple electronics. Similarly, converting an RS232C output to the required 5 milliamp MIDI current loop type is very easy. So why has this method not been adopted more widely? Almost certainly because MIDI operates at a baud rate of 31250 baud, which is not a standard RS232C rate. The serial port circuitry used in the Amiga is such that virtually any required baud rate can be set, and 31250 baud is certainly achievable. Most other computers have serial port hardware that is much less obliging, with only the standard rates being supported. In fact not all the standard rates are supported in some cases.

As a matter of interest, the original MIDI specification had the baud rate as 19200 baud, which is the highest standard rate for RS232C interfaces. This was deemed too slow for multi-channel sequencing of musical instruments though, and was raised to 31250 in the specification that was finally adopted.

Multiple MIDI

On some MIDI interfaces you will find that there are several output sockets. In most cases these all carry the same signal, and are intended as a means of coupling the output of the interface to a number of instruments. This method of connection, as depicted in Figure 3.6 is called the star system. A few MIDI interfaces have true multiple outputs, where each of two or more outputs can be individually controlled. For most purposes one MIDI output is sufficient. MIDI provides up to 16 channels, which means that 16 instruments can be simultaneously controlled. This may seem like a lot, which it is, but on the other hand most modern MIDI instruments are multi-timbral and are capable of acting as a number of 'virtual' instruments. In other words, each voice of the

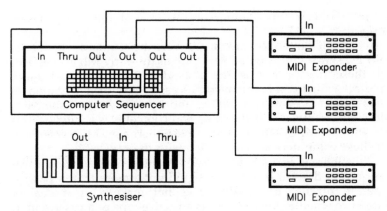

Figure 3.6 A MIDI controller having multiple outputs enables the star method of connection to be used

instrument can act virtually as a separate instrument, playing its own sound and its own set of notes. With most instruments capable of operating on six or eight channels, and some providing 16 channel operation, in a multi-instrument setup you can quickly run out of MIDI channels.

Multiple MIDI interfaces are quite rare at present, but seem likely to become more common as sophisticated MIDI equipped instruments become cheaper, and instruments which can use a large number of MIDI channels become more common. At present these interfaces are mainly produced by software companies for use with their up-market sequencer programs, offering as many as four separate outputs and some 64 channels in some cases.

Active or passive

There are two forms of MIDI interface — active and passive types. A passive MIDI interface is one which simply provides a means of communication between the computer and the MIDI instruments. Most add-on MIDI interfaces are of this basic type. An active MIDI interface has some on-board electronics to aid the software in the computer in handling MIDI data. Built-in ports of a computer are normally supported to a significant extent by the operating system. The idea of an active MIDI interface is to provide the same sort of support, thus compensating for the lack of operating system support.

Active MIDI interfaces are rare, but are the standard type for the IBM PC series and compatibles. One of the early MIDI interfaces for these machines was the Roland MPU-401, an advanced interface with an on-board microprocessor. Full documentation on this interface was made available, and it soon became a standard. Most MIDI software for the IBMs and compatibles is intended for use with the MPU-401, and most of the alternative MIDI interfaces for these computers are compatible with the MPU-401.

While there is undoubtedly some advantage in having an active interface, it does of course cost significantly more than a passive type. In practice it probably does not make a great deal of difference whether the interface is an active type or a passive unit. The quality of the software used with it is a much more significant factor in determining the quality and usefulness of the system. Something that is a crucial point to bear in mind is that there is not always compatibility between every piece of MIDI software and every add-on MIDI interface available for a particular computer. Some unofficial standards have emerged for some computers, but it is always advisable to check compatibility with the software and (or) hardware manufacturer before buying anything.

MIDI thru and thru

MIDI has the usual input and output sockets, but there is also a third type in the form of the THRU socket. This is an output, and it merely provides a replica of any signal received on the input socket. The idea behind this is to enable a number of instruments to be fed from a MIDI interface, even if it is equipped with only a single output socket. This can be achieved using the 'chain' method of connection, as shown in Figure 3.7.

In theory you can connect as many units as you like together in this manner. In practice the signal tends to be degraded slightly as it makes each trip from an IN socket to a THRU type. This can result in so-called 'MIDI delays'. It is unlikely that the problem is due to a significant delay through the series of instruments. The measurements I have made have never shown up a significant delay from an IN socket to a THRU type. The real problem is almost certainly one of the signal becoming progressively distorted until it can no longer be decoded properly. This can cause

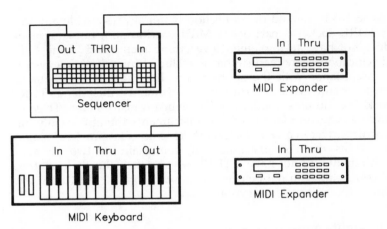

Figure 3.7 THRU sockets enable the chain method of connection to be used

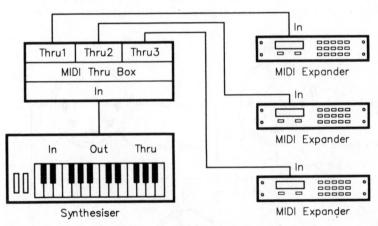

Figure 3.8 Using a THRU box to enable the star system to be used

problems such as the wrong notes being played, and notes being left droning. Probably few of us will own a sufficient number of instruments for this to become a problem. However, if necessary a single MIDI output can be connected to a THRU box. This provides a number of THRU sockets so that the star method of connection can then be used, as per Figure 3.8.

59

The chain method of connection is not always usable anyway. A THRU socket is part of the MIDI specification, but equipment does not have to implement everything mentioned in the MIDI specification. Any feature that is included must be implemented in accordance with the specification, but there is no minimum requirement. Most rack-mount instruments include a THRU socket, as do most modern MIDI keyboard instruments. They are often absent on older keyboard instruments though. If only one instrument lacks a THRU socket there is no great problem. Simply use it as the last instrument in the chain. If two or more instruments do not have a THRU socket, then the chain method of connection can not be used. You must obtain a THRU box and utilize the star system of connection.

The right connections

The standard connector for MIDI ports (of whichever type) is a 5 way (180 degree) DIN socket. Connection details for all three types of MIDI port are shown in Figure 3.9. Although the socket is a 5-

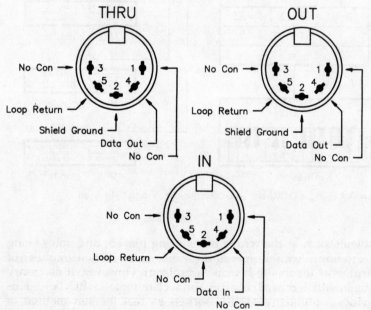

Figure 3.9 MIDI port connection details

way type, only two or three of the terminals are used. Two terminals carry the 5 milliamp current loop signal, and on an input these are the only two terminals that are connected. On outputs and THRU sockets a third terminal provides an earth connection point. MIDI cables should use twin screened lead, and this third connection connects to the screening. This prevents radio interference from being radiated from the connecting leads. Note that the screen connects to a terminal of the socket which is unconnected internally at MIDI inputs. Remember that MIDI inputs have opto-isolation, and internally connecting the earth lead at an input would bypass this isolation and the protection it affords.

Another form of connector is permitted by the MIDI standard, and this is the higher quality three way XLR type. In practice these seem to be little used. The MIDI standard stipulates that any manufacturer who uses XLR connectors must make available adaptors to permit ordinary DIN type MIDI leads to be used with their equipment.

MIDI interconnections are as straightforward as those of RS232C serial interfaces are convoluted. Having separate input and output sockets helps to simplify things, as does the lack of any handshaking. All MIDI equipment should be designed to be able to keep up with a continuous stream of instructions and data. You may sometimes encounter references to handshaking in MIDI systems, but this is a form of software control that is only implemented occasionally, and with a special category of MIDI message.

This handshaking works on the basis of a code being sent from the sending equipment to the receiving one to ask if it is ready to receive data. When a suitable acknowledgement signal is sent by the receiving device, the transmitting unit commences to send data. If the receiving equipment starts to get overloaded it sends a message to the transmitting device which causes it to temporarily halt the flow of data. Transmission is resumed when another acknowledgement message has been received. This handshaking takes place using messages sent over the data lines, and no additional connecting wires or hardware are required. As a point of interest, software handshaking of this type is sometimes used with RS232C serial systems.

If you are handy with a soldering iron it is not difficult to make up your own MIDI leads. Figure 3.10 gives details. Provided the lead is only a few metres long, virtually any type of twin screened cable should suffice. For long cables a high quality type might be needed, and note that MIDI is only guaranteed to operate at ranges of up to 15 metres.

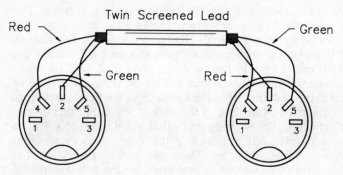

Figure 3.10 Connections for a diy MIDI lead

Dotty characters

When setting up a computer music system the two most important types of peripheral you will need to buy are the instruments themselves, and a printer. Instruments are covered in a chapter of their own, but the basics of printers will be covered here. A printer may not be *necessary*, and this depends on the type of musical application you have in mind. If the system will be used purely for sequencing there may be no need for a printer, but if you will want to print out scores, do some word processing, or anything where printed out copies will be needed, a printer is obviously essential. The usefulness of a computer system is greatly enhanced if it is equipped even with one of the cheapest printers available.

The most popular type of printer is the 'dot-matrix' type. This has a print head which moves along the paper, printing each character, and a carriage which winds the paper up line by line. The print head has a vertical row of nine pins, and these are hammered into an inked ribbon held just in front of the paper. Obviously vertical columns of nine dots do not produce text characters, but the idea is for only certain of the pins to actually be used each time the print head is hammered against the ribbon. Also, each text character is made up from several columns of dots printed side by side. By using suitable patterns of dots it is possible to produce reasonable likenesses of text characters. Figure 3.11 shows a few examples.

Dot matrix printers have the advantages of being reasonably inexpensive, and giving reasonably rapid results. My dot matrix

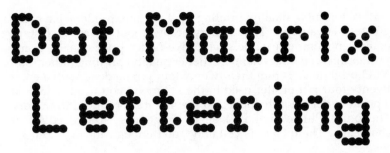

Figure 3.11 An example of dot matrix letters using a maximum height of nine dots. By using overlapping dots it is possible to achieve much higher quality

printers can manage 180 cps (characters per second), and are by no means the fastest printers of this type. However, when printing at maximum speed they produce rather poor quality results. You do not need to look particularly hard in order to see that the letters are made up from dots.

Virtually all dot matrix printers have an 'NLQ' (near letter quality) mode which gives much better print quality. The quality is usually comparable to that of one of the cheaper typewriters when used with a fabric ribbon. The higher quality is in part obtained by having each column of dots printed twice. First it is printed in the usual place, and then fractionally offset to one side. The paper is then moved up by a fraction of an inch and the dots are printed again. This fills in the gaps between the dots and gives much improved results. If the print is scrutinised very carefully the individual dots will probably not be visible as such, but the characters will have slightly ragged edges.

The price paid for this increased print quality is much reduced speed. Printing all those extra dots takes time, and the NLQ print speed is likely to be about one quarter of the 'draft' print speed. Some of the more recent dot matrix printers obtain both high printing speed and good quality by using a 24 pin printhead. These are arranged in two vertical rows of twelve pins, with one set placed a little higher than the other. The speed of a 24 pin printer in draft mode is not much different from that of a good nine pin type, and is actually slower in some cases. The quality is much better though, with more and smaller dots. The draft quality of the best 24 pin printers seems to be better than the NLQ print quality of some cheap nine pin printers.

It is for high quality printing that 24 pin printers have the greatest advantage. They are typically about twice as fast as equivalent nine pin models, and give better print quality. Some printer manufacturers claim LQ (letter quality) printing rather than NLQ print quality from their twenty four pin models. With a good twenty four pin printer used in the LQ mode you need to look at a printout very closely indeed to see that it is produced from dots. The only tell-tale sign is a slight raggedness to the edges of characters. The quality is certainly good enough for most purposes.

These 24 pin printers are certainly superior to the nine pin variety, but they are also substantially more costly. Originally the cheapest 24 pin types were around double the cost of comparable nine pin ones. The increasing popularity of these printers has resulted in a narrowing of the gap, but you are still likely to pay at least 50% extra in order to get the advantages of a 24 pin machine.

Daisy wheels

Probably the best quality printout currently available is that from a daisy wheel printer, particularly one that is used with a carbon ribbon. This is a ribbon which is made from thin plastic (like magnetic recording tape) with a coating of special ink. This gives very crisp characters, but is a little expensive. This type of ribbon is more costly to buy, and has a more limited lifespan. It is not wound to and fro between the two spools like a conventional fabric ribbon. Once the ribbon has been used once it is thrown away.

A daisy wheel printer obtains its picturesque name from the fact that the type faces are on spokes which emanate from a small wheel, which I suppose looks vaguely daisy-like. In operation the wheel rotates until the desired character is at the top, and then a simple hammer mechanism bangs it against the ribbon and paper. As the characters are not produced from dots the print quality can be very high, and is probably more dependent on the paper and ribbon qualities than on the printer's mechanism. Results are certainly as good as those from typewriters, and many typewriters actually use daisy wheel mechanisms.

Although the cost of daisy wheel printers was once quite high, it is now similar to that of dot matrix printers. They seem to have dropped markedly in popularity over the past few years though, and there are good reasons for this. They provide good print quality, but are less impressive in other respects. They are relatively noisy, and in many cases produce large amounts of vibration. They are also slow, with print speeds that are usually only about ten to twenty characters per second. There is no draft mode to permit quick printouts where high quality is of no importance. They are less flexible in terms of changing print styles, such as changing to a greater number characters per inch or printing italic letters. On the other hand, changing to a different font style is usually just a matter of changing to a different daisy wheel (although some recent dot matrix printers seem to be equipped with a number of built-in fonts that are easily selected).

We will shortly consider the subject of graphics printing, and this is one respect in which daisy wheel printers are really weak. The advertising literature for daisy wheel printers often boasts graphics printing capability, and it is indeed quite possible with many printers of this type. Quite high resolution graphics are possible in some cases. However, the advertisements tend to be very economical with the truth. The standard method of producing graphics with a daisy wheel printer is to use the fullstop character to print thousands of dots from which the picture is formed. Bearing in mind the slow printing speed of daisy wheel printers, it should be obvious that producing a complex picture in this way could take a very long time indeed. It could take hours in fact! Worse than this, graphics programs do not normally include any support for output to daisy wheel printers. In practice they are best regarded as only for high quality text use.

Dotty drawings

In contrast to the graphics capability of daisy wheel printers, dot matrix types are mostly very good. Some quite high quality results can be produced, and printout times are reasonably short. In most cases it is not so much the speed of the printer that determines printout times, it is governed more by the time taken for the program to work out the data to send to the printer. Things can be very slow when using an eight bit computer, and if you are going to do a lot of graphics work there is a considerable advantage in using a sixteen bit computer.

The main point to watch when choosing a graphics printer is whether or not the printers you are considering are compatible with the software you will be using. Some programs have drivers for long lists of printers, but in many cases the choice is limited to a few of the more popular models of the day. This is less restrictive than you might think, because there are normally drivers available for some printers in the popular Epson range. Many of printers from other manufacturers have Epson compatible graphics modes. If you are likely to use a printer for graphics use, there is a lot to be said in favour of having a fully Epson compatible type. This virtually guarantees compatibility with programs that have graphics output capability.

Dot density

When I first tried using a dot-matrix printer for graphics purposes, which was not all that many years ago, results were very poor indeed. Continuous lines looked like dot-dash lines, solid areas of black had white streaks and were basically pale grey, and diagonal lines had pronounced stepping. I put this down to inadequacies in the printer at first, but over the years as better software came along, the graphics from the printer seem to improve quite dramatically.

There are two factors which led to this apparent improvement in the performance of the printer. The more minor of these is that some of the early graphics software was less than 100% effective in working out where all the dots should go. Printed results often lacked accuracy. Although printers can operate at much higher resolutions than most monitor screens, many graphics programs only printed out at the screen resolution. They provided what is called a 'screen-dump'. Graphics software which only prints out at screen resolution is still far from rare, but in some cases the printer driver programs have refinements which provide smoother lines, and generally better looking results.

The main reason for the lack of quality in many cases is the use of the printer's lowest resolution graphics mode. Epson nine pin printers have three graphics modes, which are single, double, and quad density. These are comparable to the three text modes available on many printers, and are produced by the same multi-strike processes. The maximum resolution provided by quad density on an Epson FX/RX series printer is 240 by 216 dots per inch, which can provide quite reasonable results. There is still stepping in diagonal lines, and curves tend to be a bit jagged, but you need to look fairly closely at printouts in order to see these imperfections.

24 pin printers can produce printouts which are just that bit more precise than those from nine pin printers. The difference is most noticeable on material that has a lot of fine detail, or some

very small text. On graphics which lack these the difference can be barely noticeable. In some cases the nine pin printout may look better. Fine lines produced by a 24 pin printer are often a bit too thin, and the more solid looking lines from quad density nine pin outputs can give better looking results in some cases.

Once again, compatibility with software must be kept in mind. Twenty four pin printers are becoming more and more popular, but some software producers seem to have been a bit slow in responding to this development. If you wish to use a twenty four pin printer with a graphics program, make quite sure that it has a suitable printer driver. As with nine pin printers, your chances of finding a suitable driver are much better if your printer is fully graphics compatible with Epson models. You can use a 24 pin printer with nine pin graphics output, but results are usually quite poor. At best, the drawing is stretched vertically by about 25 percent, and is rather lacking in dot density. In some instances things seem to go radically wrong, with the paper being advanced only one pin at a time instead of 24 pins at a time. This gives a very squashed and unusable printout. A 24 pin printer is not really suitable for graphics use except where the software has a driver specifically for this type of printer.

24 pin graphics output is generally in either a low density mode or a high density type, with no intermediate density available. In my experience the low density output is too low in quality to be of much use, even for checking purposes, but the high density output is suitable for most purposes.

Light fantastic

If you require the ultimate in computer printer quality for either text or graphics, and the fastest printing speed, a laser printer is what you need. These do not use any form of impact printing, and are based on photocopier technology. Whereas a photocopier uses a photographic image of an existing document, a laser printer uses a very narrow beam of laser light to build up an image. This is done using a high speed scanning process with the laser beam being switched on in brief pulses so that light is directed only at the appropriate areas of the page. A few printers use a special light emitting diode (LED) instead of a laser beam, but these LED printers seem to be very rare these days. There are also printers of this general type which make use of liquid crystal technology (as used in liquid crystal displays). Again, these are still relatively rare.

In either case, the system relies on an electrostatic charge to hold toner powder on the paper, but only in areas which have not been subjected to the light beam. If we consider the process in highly over-simplified terms, a powerful static charge is placed onto a drum, and is consistent over the surface of the drum. The pulsed light beam is then fired at the drum and used to produce the required image in the form of charged and uncharged areas. The paper is then rolled onto the drum, and assumes the same charge pattern of the drum. The paper is taken over the toner powder which is attracted onto the areas of the paper which are charged. A thermal process is used to melt the toner powder and fix it to the paper. Do not use headed note paper in a laser printer if the printing is made from plastic ink. The thermal process can melt the ink and produce some very messy results.

This method is really a form of dot matrix printing, with the image being produced from dots of light. Most low cost laser printers use a resolution of 300 dots per inch in both planes, giving excellent quality text and graphics. The term 'low cost' is perhaps not entirely correct, since laser printers cost substantially more than dot matrix types. At one time they were only intended for office and not home use. Laser printers were large, heavy and cost upwards of £1000. Recently some smaller, lighter units in the £500 to £1000 price category have been introduced. These print more slowly than the more expensive models (about 4 pages per minute instead of 6 to 8 pages per minute). They are still quite fast in general printer terms though and offer the same high quality as the faster models. Most programs now support Hewlett Packard Laserjet printers, or compatible laser printers, which in practice means virtually all the lower cost laser printers. If you can afford a laser printer you are unlikely to be disappointed with the results, and they are definitely worth investigating.

These days there is an inexpensive alternative to laser printers in the form of ink-jet printers. As the name implies, these printers produce the images using minute jets which squirt dots of ink onto the paper. Some of these only offer resolutions that are comparable to dot matrix printers, but the Hewlett Packard Deskjet series (plus a few others) offer resolutions of 300 dots per inch or thereabouts. These provide similar results to laser printers for around £300 or so, and are now supported by most programs. At one time ink-jet printers suffered from reliability problems, with the jets tending to clog rather too frequently. Modern ink-jet printers seem to be very much better, and I have obtained trouble free results over the last year or so using one of these printers.

Mice and men

For many sixteen bit computers, such as the Atari ST and Commodore Amiga series, a mouse is part of the standard system. No mouse is included with many computers though, including virtually all eight bit machines. The importance of a mouse, or lack of it, depends entirely on the software you will be running. Some text based programs have provision for operation with a mouse, but programs of this type are almost always perfectly usable without one. There may be little advantage in using one, and many users considers a mouse out of place when used with most text based programs.

The situation is very different with graphics based programs, which includes many music applications programs such as sequencers, visual editors, and notation programs. A mouse can make these programs very much quicker and easier to use, and in some cases programs can *only* be controlled properly if the system is equipped with a suitable mouse.

If you buy software which requires or benefits from the use of a mouse, and your computer is not one which is supplied with a mouse as standard, than compatibility is something that has to be considered. The first potential problem is that a computer which is not supplied with a mouse is unlikely to have a mouse port. Mice for such a computer might not all be designed to fit the same port. Even if they are, there is still plenty of scope for designers to produce totally incompatible mice. In practice there are unofficial standards for most computers, and software that can operate with a mouse will mostly operate with any mouse available for the computer concerned. As always where there is any doubt about compatibility, check with the software and (or) hardware manufacturers before parting with any money.

There is a potential problem with mouse compatibility in that some have two buttons while others are equipped with three. In practice most programs only seem to utilize one or two mouse buttons, and any third button may prove to be unnecessary. On the other hand, I have encountered one or two programs for the IBM PC series that require a three button mouse, or are easier to use with a three button type. Once again, it is advisable to check on compatibility before actually buying anything.

You will sometimes see mice described as 'optical', 'mechanical', or 'opto-mechanical'. Optical mice are the least common, but are very good. They have two very bright light emitting diodes in their bases, plus a couple of photo-cells. If you look at the underside of an optical mouse you will see light only from one of the LEDs — the other one provides an invisible infra-red output. A mouse of this type must be used on its special pad, which has a reflective surface marked with dark lines, graph-paper fashion. The horizontal and vertical lines are of different colours. One set of lines is detected by one LED and photocell, while the other set are detected by the second LED and photocell. As the mouse is moved around the pad the photocells produce pulses as they pass over the lines, and after these have been given some electronic processing they are passed on to the computer. Software in the computer decodes these pulses into a form that applications programs can use as an indication of the direction in which the mouse has moved, and how far it has been moved.

A mechanical mouse is fitted with a weighted rubber ball which protrudes slightly through a large hole in the base of the unit. As the mouse is moved around, the ball rotates. There are two rods in the mouse which are in turn rotated by the movement of the mouse. One rod is activated by movement from side to side, while the other only responds to movement backwards and forwards. A simple electromagnetic device is used to convert the rotation of the rods into pulses that are processed and fed to the computer. An opto-mechanical mouse is broadly similar, but a simple opto-mechanical device is used to convert the rotation of the rods into electrical pulses. Neither of these types of mouse is as maintenance free as the optical type, but occasional cleaning of the moving parts is all that is needed to keep them in good working order.

Tablets

Digitizing tablets provide an alternative to mice. These have what looks very much like a mouse, but it is fitted with a lens and cross-hairs sight and often has four buttons. This is usually called a 'puck' or a 'cursor' rather than a mouse. It is used on a largish (usually about A4 to A3 size) board, and the original application was for tracing existing drawings into a computer. It is for this reason that the puck includes the simple sight — it enables drawings to be accurately traced. Most digitizers can be used with a pen-like pointing device instead of the puck.

There is a crucial difference between a mouse and a digitizer in that a mouse is relative and a digitizer is absolute. In other words, a mouse simply indicates movement by a certain amount and in a certain direction. The digitizer indicates to the computer the position of the puck, and as the puck is moved around, a series of new positions are sent to the computer. This operates using a simple system of co-ordinates, and in most cases gives tremendous accuracy. It is not uncommon for a digitizer to be able to indicate absolute positions to the nearest thousandth of an inch. Even where a high level of precision is lacking, a digitizer is still more versatile than a mouse.

A digitizer can be used as an alternative to a mouse with some programs, but it may bring no advantages over using a mouse. It may simply provide a means of moving the cursor around the screen and clicking icons and menu items. Some programs have better support for digitizers, with part of the tablet being assigned to cursor control, and the rest being used for menus (which are marked onto a template fitted on the tablet). This does have definite advantages over a mouse and on-screen menus. The most obvious of these is that none of the screen's resolution needs to be wasted on menus and menu bars, it can all be used for the graphics you are producing. Perhaps less obviously, a large number of menu items can be accommodated by most digitizers, so that every function of the software is almost instantly accessible. Learning to find your way around a tablet menu can take a while, but once mastered it becomes possible to operate the program very quickly and easily. As a point of interest, the diagrams in this book were produced using a computer drawing program controlled in this way.

Unfortunately, few programs have any proper support for a digitizing tablet. It is probably not worthwhile using a digitizer as a mouse, because the most expensive mice are substantially less expensive than the cheapest digitizers. On average, digitizers are probably about five to ten times more expensive than mice.

Plotting

At one time it was not unusual to use a plotter to produce hard copy from the few graphics oriented music programs that existed. These days few music programs have any form of plotter output, and I have not actually encountered any that do in recent years. Presumably most users prefer to use printers which are substantially cheaper, and give reasonable results. Lack of plotter support is perhaps a shame, since they can produce very high quality graphics. A plotter is simply a piece of equipment that draws on paper, drafting film, etc., using a pen. A sort of mechanical draughtsman in fact. The resolution is generally much better than that of a printer, even a laser type. If the software you use does not support any plotters, then their high quality output is of only academic importance.

Modems

It is perhaps worth mentioning modems, which are a fairly popular type of peripheral, although they have never really achieved anything like the degree of popularity that many have predicted. A modem converts the signal from an RS232C port into tones which can be fed down ordinary telephone lines, and it also decodes tones received via the phone system from another modem. It therefore provides a means for communication over the telephone system using two computer systems. There are enormous bulletin board systems that can be accessed via a modem and telephone system, and these mostly contain information on specialist areas of computing. They often permit users of the system to swap ideas and information.

The usefulness of a modem depends largely on whether or not you will be able to access useful sources of information, and contact others with similar computing interests. As technology has improved, the rate at which data can be exchanged using a modem has increased. This has resulted in a steady increase in the number modem 'standards', and you need to be careful when buying a modem. It must be compatible with your computer, you must be able to obtain suitable software for it, and it must be capable of operating with the systems you will wish to access. This is an involved subject, and one which should be studied in-depth before buying a modem.

4 Real computers

So far we have considered the world of microcomputers in broad terms, with only occasional references to real products. In this chapter we will take a brief look at the popular microcomputers currently available, paying particular attention to their suitability for music applications.

It is only fair to point out that things are not static in the world of microcomputers, and the information provided here reflects the situation when this piece was written. You really need to study some recent computer and electronic music magazines in order to discover the current situation regarding precise specifications of computers and software availability. On the other hand, things do not change as rapidly as you might think, and much of the information provided here should remain in force for some considerable time. Several of the popular computers on sale today have been on sale, in much the same form, for several years. Even most of the 'new' computers have actually been available for about three years or more! Totally new computers are a rare species these days. Changes in the specifications of existing computers or enhanced versions of established models being introduced are both frequent occurrences.

Eight or sixteen bits?

The early home computers used eight bit microprocessors. In other words, they were based on microprocessors that operated on data one byte at a time. Most eight bit microprocessors can handle sixteen bits of data internally, but they are eight bit processors in that they can only take in data and output it one byte at a time.

Many of these early eight bit computers are now well and truly obsolete, and have been out of production for many years. Some of them are still available today, albeit in what are often substantially modified forms. Early eight bit computers were usually supplied with quite modest amounts of memory in their standard forms. These days they mostly seem to have 64 k or 128 k as standard. Although they have been much improved in some respects, these eight bit machines are basically the same as the original versions, and do not have any more computing power than the originals.

The more recently introduced computers are of the sixteen bit variety. These take in and output data two bytes at a time, but internally they are usually capable of 32 bit processing. I suppose that a change from eight/sixteen bit to sixteen/thirty two bit processing may not seem like much of an advance, giving only twice the computing power. In reality matters are not quite as simple as this. If you look at the maximum values that can be handled using these various numbers of bits, things look very different. Eight bits provide a maximum value of 255. With sixteen bits the maximum value rises to 65535, and thirty two bits provides such a large maximum number that the eight digits on my calculator are unable to cope with the problem.

Where large numbers must be manipulated a sixteen bit microprocessor has a tremendous advantage over an eight bit type. Where data only needs to be manipulated eight bits at a time (or less) there is no obvious advantage in using a sixteen bit processor. There can be a slight disadvantage in that sixteen bit processors need a lot of multi-byte instructions, which take up more RAM and generally make things a little less efficient. On the other hand, the speed at which the microprocessor operates has to be taken into account.

Clocking on

Microprocessor speeds are normally given as so many megahertz (MHz). This is the speed of the clock, which is an electronic circuit that provides a regular train of pulses to the microprocessor. A clock speed of 1 MHz means that the clock provides one million pulses per second. Things can be a bit confusing here, because there are few microprocessors that operate on the basis of one instruction per clock cycle. Some microprocessors require more clock cycles per instruction than do others, and different instructions require different numbers of clock cycles to execute. If one computer has a 6502 microprocessor operating at 2 MHz, and another has a Z80A processor running at 4 MHz, the one using the Z80A is not necessarily the more powerful. In fact the one using the 2 MHz 6502 is likely to be the faster of the two, because the 6502 uses far fewer clock pulses per instruction than does the Z80A.

Where two computers have the same microprocessor, but one has a higher clock speed than the other, then the one using the higher clock speed should run the faster. At least, with all other factors being equal, the one with the faster clock should run correspondingly faster. In practice all other factors may well be extremely unequal. Some computers are designed with minimal hardware to back up the microprocessor, with a lot of functions either absent, or implemented using little or no hardware plus software routines. This has the advantage of cheapness, but it results in the microprocessor running a lot of background tasks and having relatively little time left for carrying out instructions in applications programs. If you find that applications programs seem to run much more smoothly on one computer than they do on another one having a similar basic specification, the most likely cause is that one of the computers has more and better support hardware than the other one.

In practice, sixteen bit computers operate with substantially higher clock rates than eight bit types. Even given that they require more clock pulses per instruction in many cases, this still tends to give them a speed advantage when compared to eight bit processors. This is true even when the computer is undertaking simple byte-sized operations. Of course, when undertaking complex processing the speed advantage of sixteen bit computers is massive. Comparisons are difficult since the capabilities of both types of computer vary enormously from one example to another. However, the average improvement is probably a factor of at least ten, and probably more than this.

It should be pointed out that the sixteen bit internal processing of eight bit microprocessors does not preclude them from handling complex calculations. It simply complicates matters because data can only be manipulated sixteen bits at a time, with only eight bit transfers to and from memory. Each calculation therefore has to be broken down into several smaller calculations plus a lot of shuffling data around.

Eight bit machines

Commodore 64/128

The Commodore 64 and its derivatives such as the Commodore 128 have been popular with musicians due to the machines' excellent sound chip. This was a big selling point in the pre MIDI era, but is probably not of primary importance these days. Nevertheless, with a large number of these computers in the hands of users who were interested in music applications, a substantial amount of music software was produced for them. When MIDI came along some excellent software packages were produced for these computers. There is no built-in MIDI port, but add-on MIDI interfaces are readily available. In terms of raw computing power, the 64's 6510 microprocessor (a derivative of the better known 6502 type) run at just under 1 MHz makes it less powerful than most of the competition. It has some good support chips though, and seems powerful enough to produce some good results. One problem with these computers is a lack of built-in standard interfaces. For a budget system the Commodore 64/128 would seem to be well worthy of consideration.

Amstrad CPC range

Although they were much later entries into the eight bit computer world than their main competition, the Amstrad CPC range of computers have achieved considerable success and are well supported. This includes add-on MIDI interfaces and software. These computers have the reasonably powerful 4 MHz version of the popular Z80 microprocessor, together with some reasonable support hardware. A parallel interface is one of the standard ports, but a serial interface is an optional add-on. These computers are competitively priced, especially when you take into account that they are normally sold complete with a colour or monochrome monitor and a built-in cassette recorder. The CPC128 version includes a built-in 3 inch disk drive in place of the cassette recorder.

Spectrum

The Sinclair Spectrum has been made in various versions over a number of years, one or two of which are still produced. Some of the later versions are equipped with a MIDI interface. Most of these computers have been very much made down to a price, and they are not the most powerful of 8 bit computers either. Consequently, they are considerably less than ideal for use as the basis of sophisticated MIDI system. In fact it has to be pointed out that none of the 8 bit computers will give results that genuinely rival a low cost 16 bit machine. Unless you are operating on a very tight budget, and an adequate 8 bit system can be obtained at very low cost, a setup based on a 16 bit computer is certainly a better prospect.

Sixteen bits

The power of modern sixteen bit computers is very impressive, and when it is combined with the ingenuity of the best software writers it is amazing what can be achieved. Apart from their increased processing power, an important factor in favour of sixteen bit computers is the greater screen resolution they generally provide. This can give much more detailed screen displays which are a definite advantage for many types of music software.

Atari ST

The popular Atari 520STFM and 1040STFM computers (plus their slight variants) are powerful computers which are based on a 8MHz 68000 microprocessor. There are up-market versions of these computers, called the Mega STs. The ordinary STs have the keyboard and main computer as a single unit, whereas the Mega STs are of the traditional three box variety (keyboard, main unit, and monitor). The other main difference is that the Mega STs have more memory. The 520STFM and 1040STFM have 512k and 1M respectively, while the Mega STs have 2M or 4M. There is a further difference in that the Mega versions are fitted with a device called a blitter. This aids speedy graphics, and is primarily aimed at programs which use animated (moving) graphics. This is not necessarily of much use in a music context, and is only of use with programs that are written to take advantage of the blitter. All models have a built-in 1M (720k formatted) disk drive, although many of the early 520 series computers were only equipped with a 500k (360k formatted) drive.

The ST computers have two multi-colour screen modes, plus an excellent high resolution (640 x 400 pixel) monochrome mode. The latter requires the special Atari monochrome monitor (or an expensive 'multi-sync' type). With the Atari monitor it provides what is widely regarded as one of the better quality displays currently on

Figure 4.1 The Atari ST computers have a built in MIDI interface and are very popular with computer musicians

offer, and at quite low cost. It is certainly one of the best computer displays I have seen, and it is well suited to computer music applications.

These days it is mainly the Atari 520ST-E and 1040ST-E computers that you will find in the shops (although some new STFMs still seem to be on sale). These look much the same as the STFM models, and are basically just modernised versions of the STFMs. They have somewhat improved sound and graphics capabilities, plus the blitter chip built- in as standard. The Mega STs have now gone out of production, and have been replaced with new computers.

These are the Falcon 030 computers, which are based on the 68030 microprocessor (a more powerful version of the 68000) running at 16MHz. These are similar in appearance to the ST 1040 series, but are actually much more potent. There are 1, 4, and 14 megabyte memory options, plus greatly improved sound and graphics. The latter includes a very useful 640 x 480 pixel 256 colour mode. MIDI ports are included in a good complement of interfaces that permit these computers to be easily used with hard disks and other sophisticated peripherals. These computers are more expensive than the models in the 520 and 1040 series, but they are competitively priced for such powerful computers. They appear to be ideal for running power-hungry MIDI applications.

The STs have been very popular amongst electronic music enthusiasts, and to a large extent this is probably due to the inclusion of an integral MIDI interface in all the ST computers, from the originals to the latest models. They are also powerful computers which are quite capable of running sophisticated music software. Note that many of the more sophisticated music programs for the STs require at least 1 megabyte of memory, and can therefore only be used with the 520 series computers if they have been given a suitable memory upgrade. The range of music software for the STs is unrivalled, and most of it is of very good quality. If you require a powerful MIDI system at a relatively low price, then I think it is fair to say that a system based on an Atari ST computer with monochrome display is still the obvious choice. If you have a bit more money to spend, then a system based on one of the more up-market STs is a good choice.

Amiga

While the Atari ST computers might be the obvious choice for music applications, they are not without some strong sixteen bit rivals. Recently the competition has strengthened somewhat. The most direct competition is from the Commodore Amiga. The original version (the A1000) is a three box system, but this has been superseded by the A500 and A/B2000. The Amiga 2000 computers are mainly aimed at business users, and it is the A500 that is aimed at home users. This has the electronics and keyboard in one box, with the power supply and monitor as separate units. There is a double sided 3.5 inch disk drive built into the main unit. The A500 has both parallel and serial ports, but it needs an add-on interface for MIDI purposes. This is normally in the form of a simple device which fits onto the serial port.

The standard amount of memory for the A500, as one might expect, is 512k. This is easily boosted to 1 megabyte by adding a memory board, and the A500 is often sold in packs which include various pieces of software plus the memory expansion board. Much of the more complex Amiga software requires 1 megabyte of RAM, and it is probably worthwhile buying the computer complete with the memory upgrade. Going beyond 1 megabyte is relatively costly, and is probably not worthwhile unless the software you will be using really requires it. There is now a slightly up-market Amiga called the A1500 (see page 43) which has twin disk drives and 1 megabyte of RAM. Later additions to the Amiga range are the 500

Plus and the 600 models. The latter has a built-in hard disk drive interface, and can take an internal hard disk drive.

Although the Amigas have the same microprocessor as the STs, but running slightly slower at just over 7MHz, they are generally regarded as the more powerful of the two series of computers. The Amigas have excellent graphics hardware which includes a powerful blitter chip as standard on all models (past and present). There are excellent multi-colour screen modes, including high resolution colour modes. Unfortunately, the modes which have high vertical resolution tend to suffer from 'flicker' problems. There are ways around this, such as using a monitor having a relatively long persistence screen, but in practice these modes do not seem to be used a great deal. The built-in sound generator is very powerful by computer standards, and it uses a three channel sampling system. Much Amiga music software makes use of the internal sound circuits, and some quite impressive results can be obtained. However, not all music software actually utilizes the internal sound generator, and most music software that does can also operate with a MIDI interface. While the sound generator is good by computer standards, it does not really compare with modern synthesisers and samplers, and MIDI is essential in order to get optimum results.

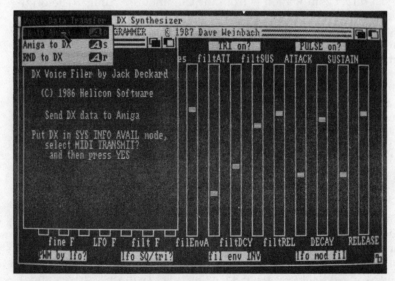

Figure 4.2 Multitasking on the Commodore Amiga. It is simultaneously running a voice filer program and a control panel type. Few computers can do this as standard

The Amiga is certainly a fine compruter in any of its versions. It has tended to be more expensive than an equivalent ST, although at present the price difference is very small, even taking into account the extra cost of a MIDI interface for the Amiga. In fact it is probably too small to be a significant factor when choosing between the two computers. In the past the ST computers had a larger software base than the Amigas, but this is probably not the case today. In terms of music software, the STs probably still have a significant lead, but the range of available Amiga software is now pretty large. The software should really be the deciding factor. Find the programs that best suit your requirements, and then buy the computer system needed to run them.

IBM PCs

Real IBM PCs (personal computers) have not been produced for some time. However, there are some modern IBM equivalents, and IBM compatible computers (or 'clones') have been produced by numerous manufacturers for many years. They are probably produced in larger numbers now than ever before. The PC world can be a bit confusing for beginners as there are now several different types of PC and what is probably dozens of manufacturers. The original PCs have a 4.77MHz 8088 microprocessor, but later PCs and clones have higher clock frequencies, and in most cases improved versions of the 8088 microprocessor. This enables them to run software written for the original PCs, but faster. In fact more than twenty times the speed of the original PCs in some cases. This is the hierarchy for the 8088 series of microprocessors, showing the normal clock frequency range for each one. The number of bits for the data bus is also shown.

Microprocessor	Clock frequency range (MHz)	Bits
8088 (or V20)	4.77 - 15	8
8086 (or V30)	4.77 - 15	16
80286	6 - 20	16
80386SX	16 - 25	16
80386	16 - 40	32
80486SX	20 - 25	16
80486	25 - 50	32

Although the fastest 80486 microprocessor at 50MHz might seem to be a little over ten times as fast as the original 4.77MHz 8088 device, the difference is actually much greater than this. The 80286 and 80386 complete most instructions in fewer clock cycles than the

8088 and 8086 microprocessors. Similarly, the 80486 is more efficient than the 80386. The fastest PCs are therefore in a totally different class to the original PCs. When dealing with PCs you will inevitably encounter references to 'XTs' and 'ATs'. These are the names of the IBM PCs that are based on the 8088 and 80286 respectively. PC clones which use the 8086 are XT class computers, while those which use 80386 or 80486 microprocessors are AT type computers (but, strictly speaking, are not true AT clones).

The IBM PCs and clones are a very different proposition to the STs and Amigas. They are primarily intended for business use, but are quite capable of running a wide range of software, including games and music applications. The computers are normally of the three unit variety, and make extensive use of internal expansion via plug-in cards. In fact they can not operate without one or two cards fitted into their expansion slots. There is no display circuitry included on the main circuit board (although a few clones include this feature), and there are a number of common display cards that can be used. The original display was a monochrome text only type which is now obsolete. The cheapest display is the Hercules type which offers monochrome text and graphics with a resolution of 720 x 348. The cheapest colour display is the CGA (colour graphics adaptor) type, but this is now largely obsolete. So is the improved version, the EGA (enhanced graphics adaptor) card. These days colour systems are almost invariably equipped with VGA (video graphics array) display cards. These have various text and graphics modes, including a very useful graphics mode which offers 640 x 480 pixel resolution in sixteen flicker-free colours. Most VGA systems now have 'super' (SVGA) modes offering resolutions of 800 x 600 and 1024 x 768 with up to 256 colours in some cases. The highest resolution suffers from a flicker problem with most monitors, but the 800 x 600 mode is good enough for most purposes.

The PCs are becoming increasingly popular for music applications. With the dramatic decreases in prices recently they seem likely to become even more popular, for MIDI and other applications. PC systems still tend to cost more than an Atari ST or Commodore Amiga plus a monitor, but will probably provide you with a more powerful computer system. The amount of PC music software available currently does not compare to that of the Atari ST and Commodore Amiga computers. But PCs are popular for MIDI applications in the USA, and plenty of MIDI PC software does exist. The amount of PC MIDI software available in the UK is increasing all the time, and there is a good chance of finding something to suit your requirements.

The PCs do not have a built-in MIDI interface, but several MIDI expansion cards are available. The nearest thing to a standard MIDI interface card is the Roland MPU-401, which is now made in more compact form as the MPU-1PC. Most PC MIDI software is designed for use with one of these cards, or a compatible card from another manufacturer. Several manufacturers produce such cards, but there is a potential snag here in that not all of these cards are fully compatible. The Roland MPU-401 is a complex piece of electronics which does more than provide basic MIDI input and output ports. It is a so-called 'intelligent' MIDI interface which actually includes its own microprocessor. This enables it to do some of the processing that would normally be undertaken by the main computer, giving a boost in performance. Not all PC MIDI cards include this built-in 'intelligence'. Such an interface card is all right for use with programs that only require a 'dumb' interface, but will obviously not work with programs that are designed to use the MPU-401's built-in processing capabilities. You therefore need to be wary of inexpensive MIDI cards which might not work with all your MIDI software. It is probably best to opt for a MPU-1PC or fully compatible card that should work with any PC MIDI programs, and will not limit your options.

Windows
Any discussion of the PCs is not complete these days unless some mention of 'Windows' is made. This is quite an involved subject, but Windows is basically just a program that you run, and then use to launch (run) applications programs such as MIDI programs. Windows provides facilities that the applications programs can use, and some programs can only be run from Windows. This now includes an increasing number of MIDI programs. If you are going to run Windows software, then it is important to have hardware that will properly support it. 8088 and 8086 based PCs are now available at very low prices, but these can only run Windows with some difficulty. Worse than this, most major Windows applications will not run at all on this type of computer. 8088 and 8086 PCs are rapidly becoming obsolete, and are now produced by few manufacturers. There are some 'bargain' PCs of this type available, but there is also an ever increasing percentage of PC software that these computers can not handle properly. Even 80286 based AT type PCs do not run some programs very well, particularly programs which

require large amounts of memory (which includes most Windows applications). Even if your current software will run properly on a relatively simple PC, there is still a lot to be said in favour of opting for one based on a 20MHz 80386SX (or better) processor. This will probably give better results now, and should run all PC software for the foreseeable future.

These days the PCs are well suited to music applications, and represent a good choice provided you can find suitable software. Due to their popularity there are now some high specification PCs selling at very competitive prices. These are ideal as the basis of a sophisticated music system if you are prepared to go a little higher up the price scale than a basic Amiga or ST system. A good budget PC MIDI system is difficult to put together since the cost of a MIDI interface is likely to be fairly high. Also, really low cost PCs may not be able to run your music software properly. If you are after a good low cost computer music system, then one based on an ST or an Amiga would probably be a better choice.

Apple Mac

The Apple Macintosh. is better known simply as the 'Mac' computer. It is actually a range of computers of varying sophistication, but they are all up-market types. They are based on the 68000 series of 16/32 bit microprocessors, like the Amigas and Atari STs. At one time these computers tended to be very expensive indeed, and were strictly for professional users with plenty of money to spend. Recently some lower cost Macs have been introduced, and this makes them much more affordable. However, they still remain in a different price category to the Amigas and STs. With the recent falls in the prices of PCs, they are also rather more expensive than all but the top notch PCs. The Macs are powerful computers which have good graphics screens. Some models have only high resolution monochrome screens (which are perfectly all right for most MIDI purposes), while the more sophisticated models have superb high resolution colour screens (which are all right for just about anything). The Macs have good MIDI potential, and there is some excellent MIDI software available for these computers. Their main drawback remains their relatively high prices. Although they are more affordable than they once were, the Macs remain beyond the reach of most MIDI users. Certainly well worth investigating though, if money is no object.

The others

This covers the most popular of the current computers, but there are definitely a couple of others that are worthy of consideration.

The Apple II computer was a very popular 8 bit computer in its day, and was much used for computer music applications. This computer has not been made for some years now though, and it now has to be regarded as obsolete. Its successor, the Apple IIGS never achieved real popularity. This is perhaps a pity, as it had a sound generator that was effectively a good quality synthesiser. Anyway, this now has to be regarded as obsolete as well.

The Archimedes computers from Acorn (the company that produced the BBC range of computers) are very powerful computers based on a 32 bit RISC (reduced instruction set computer) chip. This is a microprocessor which has a relatively small range of instructions, but with the hardware designed to perform most instructions in a single clock cycle. This permits several million instructions per second to be performed. With suitably skilful programming this enables RISC machines to perform complex tasks substantially faster than computers based on conventional microprocessors. A MIDI interface is a standard add-on for the Archimedes computers, and they should be capable of providing some outstanding results in music applications. One problem with these computers is that they are not particularly cheap, although I suppose that they offer reasonable value when their fairly advanced capabilities and taken into consideration. The main problem is that they have not achieved the same sort of popularity as the STs, Amigas, and PCs, and the amount of software for them is relatively limited. At one stage it looked as though they might offer the ultimate in MIDI performance at a reasonable price. However, at present I think that it is fair to say that in a MIDI context these computers have not lived up to their initial promise.

Software first

When setting up a computer based MIDI system do not make the classic mistake of choosing and buying a computer that seems right for the job, and then looking for software to suit your requirements. It might not exist! Ideally you would first find the software that satisfied your requirements, and would then buy the hardware needed to run it properly. In the real world there are going to be cost considerations, and you will need to look for a system as a whole that comes within your budget. There is obviously no point in giving serious consideration to software for a computer system that is beyond your means.

5 About MIDI

Reading through some of the literature on the subject of MIDI (musical instrument digital interface) you could get the impression that in the pre MIDI era there was no means of externally controlling synthesizers. This is certainly not the case, and external control of synthesizers was commonplace for many years before MIDI came onto the scene. However, it has to be admitted that the pre MIDI interfacing of electronic musical instruments tended to be rather crude. The standard method was the gate/CV type.

Problems, problems

The gate/CV method relies on two separate cables to connect the two synthesizers together. The gate signal is a logic type, and is logic 1 when a key is pressed, or logic 0 when no key is pressed. Of course, the controlled instrument does not just need to know when a key has been pressed, is needs to know which particular key has been operated. This is the purpose of the CV (control voltage) connection. Most analogue synthesizers operated using a control voltage characteristic of one volt per octave, or 83.33 millivolts (0.08333 volts) per semitone to look at it another way. Thus, if middle C was at a voltage of 3 volts, the C an octave higher would be at a potential of 4 volts, and the C a further octave higher would be at a control voltage of 5 volts.

There were three major drawbacks to this system, which never seemed likely to last when sophisticated polyphonic synthesizers started to appear. The first of these problems was a lack of true standardization. Not all instruments used the one volt per octave CV characteristic, and there were several different types of gate signal in use. Coupling two instruments together was simple enough, but there was a good chance that they would be incompatible to some degree.

Another problem was the lack of versatility in what was really a very basic method of interfacing. Note on, note off, and note value information could be exchanged, but what about keyboard velocity, pitch wheel changes, etc.? These could all be handled by further control voltage interconnections, but this would necessitate a large number of connecting cables. Comprehensive interfacing would probably require about a dozen leads to connect the two instruments together. This problem is exacerbated by the third drawback, which was that as polyphonic instruments started to appear, the gate/CV system was barely able to cope. Eight note polyphony required eight pairs of connecting cables. Obviously things could be tidied up by using one or two multi-way connecting cables, but this would still leave the system in a rather impractical form. Dozens of wires would be needed in order to implement comprehensive interfacing of this type on a polyphonic instrument. The connecting cables, even if quite short, would have been very expensive. Implementing such a system in practice would have been very difficult.

Digits out

A digital interface offered a more practical solution to the problem. Many people seem to be very confused about the precise nature of a MIDI interface. Some seem to think that the output from a MIDI port can be coupled to the audio input of a hi-fi amplifier! As we saw in Chapter 3, a MIDI interface is just a means of exchanging numbers in the range 0 to 255 which are coded into a digital form. The messages coded into these signals are quite simple, but are capable of providing comprehensive control of the sophisticated instruments of today. Note on, note off, and note values can be handled of course, but so can things such as modulation amount, pitch-wheel changes, synchronization of drum machines, and program changes. There are general purpose control signals that can be used to control practically anything the instrument designer sees fit.

There is also a special message type which gives equipment manufacturers the freedom to implement features that require large amounts of information to be exchanged, and which can not be easily implemented using the standard MIDI messages. MIDI is sufficiently versatile to permit its use with equipment such as mixers and musical effects units. It could actually be used to control practically any type of electronic device. A system of software channelling enables up to sixteen instruments to be fed individual polyphonic parts.

Although a lot of musicians seem to be under the impression that MIDI is effectively just a multi-channel version of the old gate/CV method of interfacing, there is very much more to it than this. With imaginative use of MIDI practically anything is possible.

MIDI compatibility

MIDI's versatility is its main selling point, but its true standardization comes a close second. As pointed out previously, gate/CV interfacing lacked true standardization, and connecting two instruments together often gave disappointing results. MIDI is properly standardized, and any devices which have MIDI interfaces should all work perfectly well together as an effective and fully operational system. This is true even if there are a dozen pieces of equipment in the system which each one coming from a different manufacturer.

It would be an exaggeration to claim that any two pieces of MIDI equipment could be used together with totally compatibility. MIDI interfaces are present on some very sophisticated pieces of equipment, and on some very simple items of equipment. If two devices that are very different in their capabilities are used together there is obviously going to be less than total compatibility between the two. However, they should function together as well as the limited facilities of the more simple unit permit. MIDI enables manufacturers to implement special features that can only be accessed using other pieces of gear from the same manufacturer. These features will not be available in a system that uses instruments from several different makers. It is only the special features that will not be available though, and the instruments should work very well together in all other respects.

Channels

Unless you are going to undertake MIDI programming, or designing your own MIDI hardware, you do not really need a comprehensive understanding of the MIDI codes. On the other hand, you do need to know what types of message are available, and exactly what each one can and can not do, if you wish to fully exploit MIDI systems. We will therefore consider MIDI messages in reasonable detail, but will not bother with the actual code numbers etc.

MIDI messages fall into two broad categories — the channel and system types. MIDI provides operation on sixteen channels, and these enable messages to be directed to just one instrument in a system, or with suitable instruments they can be directed to one voice of one particular instrument in the system. Only the channel messages can be used in this way. The system messages are always fed to every device in the system. Matters are complicated slightly by the use of several modes of operation. These differ only in the way channel messages are handled. Instruments do not necessarily bother to sort out messages on one particular channel, and can respond to channel messages on any channel.

It is important to understand that this method of channelling operates by having a channel number included in the first byte in each message. This 'header' byte is split into two four bit sections which are called (believe it or not) 'nibbles'. The first nibble contains the code for the particular type of message being sent, and the second one contains the channel number. One of the sixteen possible message codes is the system message type. As this does not require the second nibble for a channel number, this can instead be used to identify one of sixteen system message types (but not all sixteen codes have been implemented).

As MIDI channels only exist in the form of a number in the header byte, any device that receives messages can respond to the channel numbers or ignore them. It is this that makes the various modes of operation possible. There are five MIDI modes (including an unofficial but popular one), and these are detailed in the following section. Note that these modes are known by number and by a name. In some cases the current name is a new one, and these modes are perhaps still better known by their old names.

MIDI modes

Mode 1 (omni on/poly)
This mode ignores channel numbers, and a device in this mode will therefore respond to all the received channel messages.It is a polyphonic mode, which simply means that it can operate with more than one note at a time being played. The MIDI specification does not lay down any rules governing the minimum or maximum

number of notes that an instrument in a polyphonic mode must be able to handle. It is up to the user to ensure that instruments are not fed with more notes than they can handle. This mode is a fairly fool-proof one in that an instrument in mode 1 will respond to messages from any MIDI source, with no risk of notes being lost because something was not set up quite right on the sending equipment. It lacks versatility though, and effectively downgrades MIDI to a single channel system. Incidentally, this mode was originally called 'omni mode', and is still frequently referred to by this name.

Mode 2 (omni on/mono)
Mode 2 is similar to mode 1, but it allows only monophonic operation (i.e. only one note at a time can be played). As it provides what is really only single channel single note at a time operation it is of very limited use. It was probably included only to accommodate the few monophonic analogue synthesizers that were equipped with MIDI interfaces. It is little used in modern MIDI systems. Most modern instruments can not be set to this mode. It would downgrade a polyphonic instrument to monophonic operation, and there would consequently be little point in using it anyway.

Mode 3 (omni off/poly)
This mode, which was formerly known as 'poly' mode, is the most powerful of the four official MIDI modes. In this mode a device will only respond to channel messages that are on the correct channel, and it provides polyphonic operation. Things need to be set up a little more carefully when using this mode, as getting the transmission or reception channel set incorrectly will result in the receiving device ignoring the messages to which you want it to respond. It is a very powerful mode in that you can have up to sixteen instruments with each one being sequenced separately, and polyphonically. In other words, you can have what is effectively a MIDI controlled orchestra, brass band, or whatever, but only if you can afford all those instruments.

Mode 4 (omni off/mono)
Although mode 4 is often regarded as the most powerful of the MIDI modes, strictly speaking this is not true. It implements MIDI channels, but it permits only monophonic operation on each channel. The factor that has made this mode very popular with sequencer users is that it permits each voice of an instrument to

be assigned to a different MIDI channel. It is usually only possible to have the voices assigned to consecutive channels, but this is not really a major drawback.

The real power of this mode is obtained when it is used with a multi-timbral instrument (i.e. one which can have each voice playing a different sound). With a sixteen voice instrument set to mode 4, you once again have what is a sort of MIDI controlled orchestra or band. It is not quite as good as a number of instruments used in mode 3 though, since mode 4 restricts each channel to monophonic operation. Obviously though, one or two instruments in mode 4 is a more affordable proposition than sixteen instruments operated in mode 3. This mode was originally called 'mono' mode, and is still popularly known as such.

Multi mode

When MIDI was first designed, the four modes that were selected seemed to cover all eventualities. However, they did not leave much room for expansion, and as instruments became more sophisticated they soon outgrew mode 4. A thirty two voice instrument in mode 4 has to abandon half its voices. Even for an instrument that has sixteen or less voices, mode 4 lacks flexibility. Sixteen monophonic channels might suit your requirements, but something like four channels with four note polyphony on each one might be a better way of using up sixteen voices.

In order to overcome the limitations of the original four modes, several instrument manufacturers implemented special modes. These were given a variety of names by the equipment producers, but seem to have become known as 'multi' mode. This mode varies somewhat from one implementation to another, but there is one common factor in that it permits operation on a sort of polyphonic mode 4. Some instruments are quite restrictive, and you have to choose from a few preset voice assignments. For instance, a sixteen voice instrument in multi mode might offer eight channels with up to two notes per channel, four channels with a maximum of four notes per channel, or two channels with up to eight notes per channel.

The more flexible instruments offer what is termed 'dynamic' voice assignment. The instrument then assigns the voices in the manner which best handles the received notes, changing the voice assignments as and when necessary. As an example, assume that a sixteen voice instrument must operate on ten channels. With dynamic allocation you do not need to specify a maximum number of notes per voice, you simply assign a particular sound to each channel. If you use one note on each channel 1 to 9 and seven notes on channel 10, that should be perfectly all right as the maximum of sixteen notes has not been exceeded. If this is immediately followed by something like eight notes each on channels 1 and 2, or sixteen notes on channel 3, the system will still function properly, and without the user having to make any changes in any settings. The instrument will automatically assign its voices to make the best use of them, and everything will function perfectly provided the maximum number of notes that can be handled simultaneously is not exceeded.

Even one of the more basic versions of multi mode is highly desirable for sequencing work. The more sophisticated forms are that much more useful. They can give tremendous results from even a single instrument. Bear in mind that some recent instruments offer something like 32 note polyphony combined with six or eight note multi-timbral operation.

Although multi mode might seem to be outside the MIDI specification, and therefore something that can not be legitimately included on MIDI instruments, this is not really the case. An instrument in multi mode, as far as the MIDI controller is concerned, is a number of mode 3 instruments on different MIDI channels. The fact that the instruments are all in the same box is of no consequence. Each channel of a multi mode instrument is sometimes termed a 'virtual instrument'.

Transmission modes?

MIDI modes define the ways in which receiving devices can handle channel messages. You may sometimes encounter modes applied to the controller in a MIDI system, but this is perhaps not a fully legitimate use of MIDI mode names. If a MIDI unit transmits messages only on channel 1, then I suppose it could be said to be in mode 1 (omni on/poly). Similarly, a unit which transmits monophonically on several channels could be deemed as operating in mode 4 (omni off/mono). However, you will not normally encounter mode names when dealing with devices that only transmit MIDI data.

Getting the message

The most important of the MIDI messages are undoubtedly the note on and note off types. In both cases the header byte is followed by two data bytes. The first of these is the note value.

This provides semitone increments, the middle C is at a value of 60. A range of 0 to 127 enables more than ten octaves to be accommodated. This should be sufficient for all practical purposes, and is substantially more than most instruments can actually manage. The second data byte is the velocity value. In other words, it reflects how hard or soft the key was pressed when that note was played or released. Touch sensitive keyboards used to be quite a rarity. Fortunately, these days there are very few instruments that do not implement this feature. Where an instrument does not support touch sensitivity, this second data byte must always be included in the note on/off messages it sends. The note on velocity value is normally set to a middle value of 64, while the note off velocity value is usually 0. An instrument that does not support touch sensitivity will simply ignore the velocity data values in any note on/off messages it receives.

As an alternative to a note off message, a note on type having a velocity value of 0 can be used. I am not sure what the point of this happens to be, and have never found anyone who has a plausible explanation. Anyway, a lot of instruments now seem to use this as their standard method of switching notes off.

A touch of class

Key velocity sensing is the most common form of touch sensitivity, but some keyboards also implement aftertouch. This is where pressing a key more or less hard on long notes makes the volume increase or reduce. There are two forms of aftertouch, and the more simple of these is the overall variety. This gives a sort of average volume on all notes based on how hard the keys are depressed. Polyphonic aftertouch is a more up-market form which controls the volume of each note according to how hard its key is pressed. This is obviously a superior form of aftertouch, but it is one that has been little used in the past. In fact neither form of aftertouch has been particularly common so far. This is unfortunate, since it is impossible to mimic the playing styles of many instruments (strings and wind for example) without dynamic control provided by aftertouch. Presumably this feature was difficult and expensive to implement, as it only seemed to be included on a few of the more expensive instruments.

Fortunately, aftertouch in one form or the other is becoming more common, and is even included in some quite low cost instruments these days. The overall version is more common than polyphonic aftertouch, but even this more simple version is a considerable asset. Of course, aftertouch is not something that can only be included in keyboard instruments. MIDI expander units can and sometimes do have the ability to respond to aftertouch information. This is useful if you have a keyboard that includes this feature, since a real-time sequencer should be able to record aftertouch messages. If a recorded track is sent to a suitable expander, it will then follow the dynamic information included in these recorded aftertouch messages. Even if the system's keyboard does not have aftertouch, it could still be useful to have an expander which responds to aftertouch messages. Your software might permit manual editing of MIDI data, including the ability to add in messages such as aftertouch types. Similarly, if you undertake step-time sequencing it is possible that the software will permit dynamic control of tracks via aftertouch messages.

The overall aftertouch messages consist of the header byte plus one data byte. This data byte is simply the key pressure value. Polyphonic aftertouch requires the header byte plus two data bytes. The first of these indicates which key the message refers to, and this is the same value that is used in note on/off messages for the key concerned (e.g. 60 for middle C). The second data byte is the pressure value for that key.

All change

Program change messages are amongst the most useful of those provided by MIDI, and also rate as one of the most frequently used message types. The 'program' part of the name is perhaps a little misleading, and in this context it normally refers to a set of sound generator settings for a synthesizer. In other words, it enables the sound of the instrument to be charged via MIDI. If used intelligently this can greatly enhance the power of the system. Suppose you have a simple MIDI setup which has just one instrument, an eight voice multi-timbral type. On the face of it you are limited to eight sounds per sequence. But what if the instrument can have one hundred pre-programed sounds stored in its memory, with the ability to assign any one of these to any channel via MIDI program change messages. You can repeatedly change the sound produced by each channel, enabling dozens of different sounds to be included in each sequence if desired. There is a limit of only eight instruments being usable at any one time, but this still gives much greater flexibility than if the system is restricted to the same eight sounds throughout each sequence.

It is worth pointing out that program change messages are not only used with synthesizers to switch between sounds. They can be used with other instruments such as samplers in a similar fashion, but they can also be utilized with other MIDI controlled equipment, such as audio mixers and sound effects units. With effects units for example, each program would be a certain effect with a certain group of settings. If each sound from the synthesizer required a different effect from the effects unit, this could be easily arranged. Each program on the synthesizer would be matched with the appropriate effect under the same program number on the effects unit. Changing the sound of the synthesizer via a program change message would then automatically change the effects unit to the correct effect as well. Program changes messages are most useful when the user can specify the parameters for each program, or assign the program number for each set of parameters. Things are much more restrictive when neither of these are possible.

Program change messages are not only used when sequencing. Most synthesizers can be set so that they will transmit an appropriate program change message when the program is switched via the instrument's front panel controls. If the synthesizer is linked to an effects unit via MIDI, this unit can be made to automatically switch to the correct effect for whatever sound is selected on the synthesizer.

A program change message consists of just two bytes — the header byte and the new program number. This program number is in the usual MIDI data range of 0 to 127, but there is room for confusion here as this is not the method of program numbering used on most instruments. The program numbers usually start at 1 on synthesizers, but computer software sometimes deals in the actual MIDI data byte values. This is obviously only a minor inconvenience though. If you have software that enables program change messages to be edited into tracks, you would simply need to use a value one less than the program number you would set on the instrument in order to obtain the required sound.

Sometimes the method of program numbering is less convenient. My Casio CZ1 has two sets of push button switches that are used to select the required program. The push buttons are marked 1 to 8 and A to H, and the sixty four programs are from A-1 (MIDI program number 0) to H-8 (MIDI program number 63). When program identifications of this type are used, the manual will often include a conversion chart to make things easier when selecting programs using MIDI program change data values.

Note that although MIDI has provisions for 128 different

programs, few instruments seem to offer this many. The limit is often 64 or 100. Most instruments will simply ignore program change messages that have a program number which is higher than the maximum one supported by the instrument.

In control

MIDI has provision for control adjustments, but you need to be careful when using this feature. Apart from control number 1, which is the modulation wheel, the MIDI 1.0 specification does not lay down rules about what each control should do. There are some unofficial standards, and the detailed MIDI specification does now allocate definite functions to many of the control numbers (see Appendix 4 for a complete listing of these). With older MIDI equipment you still need to be careful though, as it might not adhere to the current scheme of things. Unless all your MIDI equipment is quite modern, there is a real risk of incompatibilities. You should bear in mind that few MIDI controllers are actually implemented on most pieces of equipment.

There are two types of MIDI control, the 'continuous' and 'switch' types. Control numbers from 0 to 63 are continuous types, while those from 64 to 95 are the switch controls. A control change message consists of three bytes, which are the header byte, the control number data byte, and finally the control setting byte. Switch type controls can only be on and off, which are selected using setting values of 0 and 127 respectively. Other values in the final byte will result in the message being ignored.

The variable controls can make use of the full 0 to 127 range in the final byte, giving up to 128 settings for each control. This type of control is used for such things as volume and filter controls, and for most purposes some 128 settings are perfectly adequate. Taking our example of a volume control, with 128 settings the volume could be varied from maximum down to the point where the signal was rendered inaudible, and there would be no noticeable change in volume from one setting to the next. In other words, the 'resolution' of the system would be sufficient for the steps in volume not to be heard as such. Changes in volume would be smooth, just as if they were produced using an ordinary volume control.

Despite this, MIDI has provision for much higher resolution. The variable controls are grouped in pairs, with control 0 matched with control 32, control 1 matched with control 33, and so on up to control 31 which is matched with control 63. The two seven bit numbers of each control are grouped together to form a fourteen bit number. This gives a setting range of 0 to 16383, which provides extremely high resolution. In fact the resolution is so high that it goes well beyond most requirements. Few MIDI instruments actually bother to implement this system, although I have encountered a few that use high resolution on one or two controls. In most cases control numbers 0 to 31 are utilized, while control numbers 32 to 63 (which would provide the 'fine tuning') are just ignored.

In the mode

As you may have noticed, control numbers from 69 to 127 are not used for either continuous or switch type controls. Many of these control numbers are, as yet, unassigned to any purpose. They may be put to use in the future. Some of them have been assigned functions, and are used for special purposes such as mode changes. This is a list of the control numbers above 95 that have so far been allocated functions.

Control no.	Function
121	Reset all controls
122	Local control on/off
123	All notes off
124	Omni mode off
125	Omni mode on
126	Mono mode on (poly mode off)
127	Poly mode on (mono mode off)

Control number 121 has only recently been assigned to the reset function, and so this feature is absent on many instruments. It simply resets all controls to their default settings (i.e. their normal settings at switch-on).

Local control refers to the normal method of playing the instrument, which in the vast majority of cases means the keyboard. Switching off local control makes it impossible to play the instrument from the keyboard, wind controller, or whatever, but it does not disable the instrument in any other respect. Playing on the keyboard still results in MIDI data being produced from the MIDI output socket, and the instrument will respond to any messages received via its MIDI input socket. In effect the

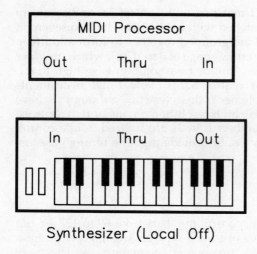

Synthesizer (Local Off)

Figure 5.1 Increasing the capabilities of a synthesizer using a MIDI processor

instrument is converted into a separate keyboard and MIDI expander unit.

This may seem to be totally pointless, but it does have its uses. As a simple example, consider the setup of Figure 5.1. Here the MIDI output of the synthesizer is being processed in some way, and then fed back to the instrument's MIDI input. Various types of processing are possible, and 'channelizing' is one possibility. Some synthesizers have a keyboard-split facility, where notes from a certain key and above play one voice of the instrument on a certain MIDI channel, while the other notes play on a different voice and MIDI channel. The two sections of the keyboard can therefore be used to play totally different sounds. This system is not limited to a two-way split, and three or more keyboard sectors and voices could be used. External MIDI processing and the local off mode provides a means of adding this facility to an instrument which does not have it built in. As we will see later, it can sometimes be helpful to use the local off facility when undertaking sequencing work. Of course, with MIDI expanders there is no local control, and this message is not implemented.

The all notes off command is not intended as the normal means of switching off notes. The MIDI specification makes it clear that it should not be used in this way. It is intended as a sort of safety feature, which can be used to switch off any notes that have been left droning as the result of a system fault. Incidentally, changes in MIDI mode also have the effect of switching off any notes that are left on at that time.

Mode changing is not accomplished by having a separate message for the selection of each mode. Instead, it is a matter of switching omni, mono and poly on or off in order to obtain the required mode. This process is quite straightforward if you think in terms of the name of each mode rather than its number.

It is worth noting that a few manufacturers seem to use some MIDI controls in a slightly less than standard manner. A non-standard method of this type is to have one of the continuous controls used to select a parameter, and then use another control to adjust this parameter. This is fine, except two consecutive control numbers around the 100 mark are sometimes used for one of these functions. If you intend to make use of MIDI controls, you really need to carefully read the MIDI specifications for your instruments in order to find out exactly how they are implemented.

Pitch wheel

Most synthesizers have two large rotary (edge-type) controls just to the left of the keyboard. One of these controls the modulation depth and the other is the 'pitch wheel'. The pitch wheel enables the pitch of the instrument to be varied either side of its normal level, so that manually controlled vibrato can be used. This could be handled in MIDI using one of the standard continuous controls, but it is deemed sufficiently important to have its own message type. The pitch wheel change header byte is followed by two data bytes. Like the standard continuous controls, two data bytes are used together in order to give increased resolution. However, whereas adjusting both data bytes of a standard MIDI control requires two messages, with a pitch wheel message the data bytes are both in a single message. This gives slightly improved efficiency, but you need to be aware of the fact that pitch wheel changes can generate vast amounts of MIDI data. Pitch wheel changes therefore need to be used with a certain amount of caution. Used to excess they can result in MIDI 'clog', which at best can result in significant changes in the timing of MIDI notes, and which at worst could probably cause the system to crash out of control. When using a sequencer a lot of pitch wheel changes can soon use up all your sequencer's memory.

System messages

Several of the MIDI system messages are concerned with the synchronization of two sequencers. This usually means the synchronization of a drum machine to the main sequencer. The drum machine is set up to produce the required drum pattern, which in most cases is a short repetitive track. MIDI system messages are then used to ensure that the drum machine starts at the right time, keeps in synchronization with the main sequencer, and stops at the right time. Although the drum machine will often be producing a short repetitive track, MIDI can synchronize quite long sequences if required.

You do not necessarily have to use the drum machine's built-in sequencer. It is possible to control everything from the main sequencer, with the drum machine being given its own MIDI channel. One channel is sufficient, as the normal way of controlling a drum machine is to have each drum sound assigned to a different note, rather than to a different MIDI channel (although a few have provision for this method of working). This central control method is beginning to gain in popularity, and some sequencers have special facilities to make it easy to produce repetitive drum tracks. Also, some synthesizers now seem to have one MIDI channel given over to a variety of drum sounds. A sort of built-in drum machine minus any sequencing capability. The advantage of using system messages to provide synchronization of the two sequencers is that all sixteen MIDI channels are left available for other purposes. The advantage of controlling everything from one sequencer is that, with a suitable sequencer, it is a more convenient way of doing things.

The basic synchronization signals are 'stop', 'start', and 'clock' signals. MIDI clock signals are not the simple electronic pulses used in conventional drum machine synchronization systems, but are single byte MIDI messages sent at regular intervals, (24 pulses per quarter note). Of course, the start and stop signals are also MIDI messages, and are again single byte types. There is also a 'continue' message, which is used after a stop signal to cause the sequence to resume where it left off. A start message will not do this, as it always starts the sequence from the very beginning.

Song pointer

The song pointer message is closely allied to the MIDI timing signals, but it not strictly speaking in the same category. It is used to take the slave sequencer (i.e. the one which is synchronizing to the MIDI timing signals) to a particular point in the sequence. This enables sequences to be started other than at the beginning of a sequence if desired. This system operates by each sequencer in the system having a counter which keeps track of the number of MIDI beats that have elapsed. The maximum value the counter can have is 16383. MIDI song pointer messages therefore require two data bytes after the header type. After using the song pointer message to set both sequencers to the desired position in the song, it is a continuous message and not a start type that is issued to start the sequence at the selected point, as explained previously.

This feature is one that is more common than it used to be, but is still not supported by all sequencers. There is a potential problem when using this facility in that some devices can move to a new point in a sequence faster than others. Ideally the continue message should not be issued until a little while after the song position message has been sent, so that all the sequencers in the system have time to set themselves to the new point in the sequence.

Song select

This is a two byte message which consists of the header byte and a single data byte which contains the new song number. It is used with sequencers that can operate with several sequences in memory. For example, a drum machine might be able to store several patterns in its memory, and you might wish to use different patterns at different points in a sequence. Provided both the drum machine and the main sequencer support song select messages, the drum machine can be set to any pattern at any time. Like program numbers, songs are numbered differently from one device (or piece of software) to another. You therefore need to take care in order to ensure that you get the pattern you require at each point in the sequence.

Reset

If a system reset message it received by a device that supports this feature, the device is set to its switch-on state. I suppose that if you ended up with some controls at the wrong settings, a system reset message might offer a quick means of getting things back to where you needed them. In practice this might not give the desired effect since the start-up settings of the instrument might not be the ones you require. Also, most pieces of MIDI equipment seem to ignore this message anyway. With a disk based instrument such as a sampler, taking the unit back to its start-up state does not seem to be very useful. Samplers are unplayable at switch-on since they have no samples loaded in memory. They must first be loaded from disk. Many modern MIDI instruments seem to make use of battery-backed RAM to hold sound data, patches, etc., so that at switch-on they carry on where they left off. Just what constitutes a reset state with one of these is debatable, but the instruments of this type I have encountered do not support the reset message anyway. The reset message is a single byte type incidentally.

Active sensing

This seems to be a feature that is rarely implemented in practice, but it appears to be a potentially useful one. The basic idea is for the controlling device in the system to periodically send an active sensing message. Periodically in this case means at least every 300 ms (0.3 seconds), but preferably not much more frequently than this so that the MIDI data stream is not unnecessarily clogged up. If a MIDI cable should become damaged so that certain devices in the system no longer receive messages from the controller, these devices will detect the problem as they will no longer receive the active sensing messages. The controlled devices then switch off their sound generator circuits so that there is no possibility of notes being left switched on.

Instruments only go into the active sensing message mode if an initial active sensing message is received. Thus, an instrument should not go into the muted state if no active sensing messages at all are received. This is just as well, as very few MIDI devices seem to be capable of sending them.

Tune request

Although this sounds like something you send in to a radio station, it is actually a form of MIDI system message. The word 'tune' in this case does not mean a melody. It means tune in the sense of tuning an instrument to set it to the correct pitch. Some synthesizers have an automatic tuning facility, whereby pressing the appropriate switch or switches results in the instrument adjusting itself for a frequency of (usually) 440 hertz when middle A is played. In other words, the instrument automatically tunes itself to standard concert pitch. The tune request message is a means of calling up this facility via MIDI.

This message does not provide any timing information to aid tuning of the instrument — it is just a simple single byte message. It simply tells the instrument to tune itself against its integral tuning reference. This would normally be very accurate indeed, so that once this message has been issued, all the instruments in the system that support this feature should be accurately in tune with each other. This is a little implemented feature though, and it is likely that nothing in your system will be able to generate or respond to this MIDI message.

System exclusive

System exclusive messages are the ones which enable MIDI equipment manufacturers to implement any special features that they can not implement using the standard MIDI messages. These messages start with the system exclusive header byte, which is followed by the code number for the manufacturer concerned. This code number is important, because it is followed by any number of data bytes and then the system exclusive end message. The meaning of the data bytes varies from one manufacturer to another, and the effect of system exclusive messages for one instrument on a different instrument could well be to scramble its sound generator settings, or something of this nature.

Obviously this eventuality must be avoided, and the manufacturer's code makes it possible to do so. Unless a device detects the correct manufacturer's code, it will simply ignore the entire system exclusive message. It is up to manufacturers to design their system exclusive message to avoid problems with messages for one model of instrument being accepted by an instrument which will interpret them incorrectly. This is often achieved by having an instrument code number, or message type code number as the third byte in the message. This enables instruments to filter out messages that have the right manufacturer's code, but are not compatible with that particular model. As an example of incompatibility, it is obviously not possible for a sampler to make sense of a dump of sound data from a synthesizer. Their methods of generating sounds are totally different, and dumps of sample data from the sampler would not make much sense to the synthesizer either.

As explained previously, MIDI system exclusive messages can be used to implement absolutely any feature that the equipment manufacturer desires. In practice these messages are mainly used to implement facilities that require large amounts of data to be transferred from one device to another. This mainly means dumps of sample data or complete sets of sound data.

There is a trend towards using system exclusive messages to permit access to individual parts of an instrument's sound generator circuits. Most modern instruments are notoriously difficult to adjust via their front panel controls, and some manufacturers produce add-on programmer units that have rows of control knobs which make it easy to rapidly adjust virtually any parameter. An alternative approach is to have a computer running a controller program, which usually takes the form of on-screen controls that can be adjusted using the mouse. In either case, access to the sound generator circuits is by way of MIDI.

This type of thing could be handled using the ordinary MIDI controls, but these days it often seems to be handled primarily using system exclusive messages. This is perhaps an unwelcome trend as it makes MIDI less universal than it might otherwise be. General purpose MIDI controllers are virtually useless with some instruments, which require dedicated controller units or software. Possibly modern instruments simply have too many adjustable parameters for the standard MIDI controls to cope.

I suppose that the inclusion of system exclusive messages at all may seem to run contrary to MIDI's main concept of a universal system that avoids equipment incompatibilities. On the other hand, there was no point in developing an interface system that was too limiting, resulting in the various manufacturers giving it up at an early stage and going their own (probably divergent) ways. Provided manufacturers resort to system exclusive messages only when they are really necessary, MIDI will still live up to its design aim of letting equipment from a variety of manufacturers operate properly together as a system.

As a point of interest, MIDI equipment producers are obliged to make available details of their system exclusive codes to anyone who wants them, and to allow free use of them. They must also leave the codes unchanged, apart from any extensions to them that they may wish to add.

Universal system exclusive

In situations where a number of equipment producers are using system exclusive messages in very much the same way, there is obviously a strong case for them getting together and agreeing on a standard way of handling things. So far this only seems to have happened once, and this was to agree on a standard method of transferring sample dumps over MIDI. By the time a sample dump standard was agreed, some manufacturers had developed their own MIDI sample dump transfer systems. Consequently, many samplers do not adhere to this method of sample transfer. With some manufacturers having their own well established methods of transferring sample dumps via MIDI, it is quite possible that the sample dump standard will never be adopted by all producers of samplers.

MIDI messages which are standardized system exclusive types are termed 'universal system exclusive' messages. This term is something of a paradox, but we know what they mean! Messages of this type operate very much like ordinary system exclusive types, but, instead of the manufacturer's code number, the second byte is the appropriate universal system exclusive identifier code.

Setting up a system

It must be possible to produce dozens of different MIDI set-ups from a small array of equipment. However, not all the possible permutations would necessarily be worthwhile. Most users opt for one of a few basic arrangements, and in most cases there is no advantage in choosing a more exotic method of interconnection.

The most basic setup for a computer based system is shown in Figure 5.2. This simply has the input and output sockets of the two

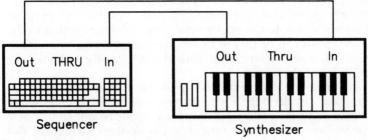

Figure 5.2 The basic sequencer/synthesizer set-up

devices cross coupled, with the THRU sockets simply being ignored. Music played on the keyboard can be recorded into the computer, and then played back again from the computer into the keyboard instrument. With something like a notation program that supports MIDI, music entered into the program can be sent to the instrument. Although this is a very simple setup, using good quality software and a modern multi-timbral instrument it can produce some very good results indeed.

The usual expansion of this basic arrangement is to add further instruments, as in the setup of Figure 5.3. This uses the chain

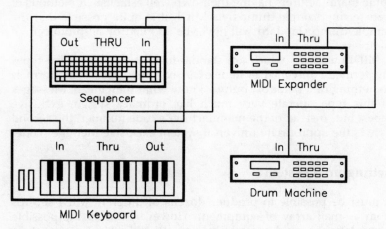

Figure 5.3 A more sophisticated system utilizing the chain connection

method of connection, but obviously the star system could be used instead if the computer has multiple MIDI outputs or a THRU box is used. This system operates in what is basically the same manner as the previous one, with the synthesizer's keyboard being used to enter sequences into the computer. Also as before, the computer can output music to the synthesizer. The difference is that in this case the music can be played by the synthesizer, a drum machine, and a MIDI expander unit. This should greatly enhance the capabilities of the system.

A common problem with a setup of this type is that when you are playing a track on the keyboard, you will hear the synthesizer's internal sound generator, but this track might be one that should be played on another instrument in the system. Remember that the signal from the keyboard appears on the computer's THRU socket (which is left unconnected) and not on its OUT socket (which feeds the other instruments in the system). These days a lot of sequencers provide a way around this problem in the form of a THRU facility. When this feature is activated, any signals received on the computer's MIDI input are echoed on the OUT socket as well as the THRU socket.

There is a potential problem here in that the synthesizer will still be directly activating its sound generator circuits from the keyboard. Also, the synthesizer will be receiving the MIDI data it is generating, which could produce a doubling up of notes. The way around this problem is to switch the synthesizer to the local off mode, so that it effectively operates as a separate keyboard and sound generator module. This feature can often not be set from the synthesizer's controls, but many sequencers can send local on and local off MIDI messages.

If your sequencer lacks the necessary facilities to handle things in this way it might be necessary to introduce a MIDI switcher into the system, as in the arrangement of Figure 5.4. This enables the

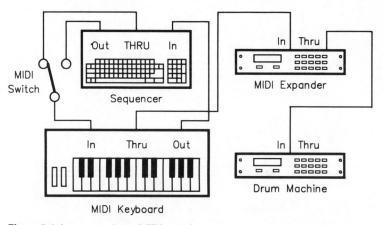

Figure 5.4 A set-up using a MIDI switch

instruments to be fed from either the THRU socket or the OUT socket of the computer. Normally the THRU socket would be used when recording sequences, and the OUT socket would be utilized when playing them back.

If you have a lot of MIDI equipment, it is easy to end up in a situation where you seem to be forever unplugging and plugging in leads in order to reconfigure the system. If this should happen, than a MIDI patchbay is the answer to the problem. This has numerous inputs and outputs, and the idea is to connect it to the INs and OUTs of everything in the system. The patchbay is then used to interconnect all these INs and OUTs in the desired fashion. A patchbay is certainly a very useful piece of equipment, but probably few systems include enough MIDI devices to make one worthwhile, and they tend to be quite expensive accessories.

6 Music software

Modern microcomputers combined with MIDI equipped electronic instruments provide tremendous music making potential. The type of system which not so long ago would have (literally) cost a fortune is now within the budget of many musicians. I suppose that the types of system which are now being used by thousands of musicians would not have been possible at all two or three decades ago. With new and improved instruments and software coming along practically every month, one can only speculate what the ultimate computer controlled MIDI system will be able to achieve.

The right one

In the meantime, the capabilities of the current software and hardware are good enough for most people's needs. In fact the range of software available for some computers, and the numerous facilities offered by many of these programs, make it difficult for the beginner to know where to start. I think it is fair to say that to some extent the massive choice of software is an illusion. There are some unique products on offer, but a substantial proportion of software is very much the same sort of thing from various software houses. Sequencers are perhaps the best example of this, with probably dozens of them available. However, they all provide the same basic function, and in use there are strong similarities between many of these programs.

There are differences though, the most obvious one being that some of these programs are very basic types with low price-tags, while others have a bewildering array of features and cost more than the computer they are running on. Some programs run faster and are easier to use than their competitors, but the main differences between programs of the same basic type are often in the extras that are included in the range of facilities. If you find two programs with similar basic specifications, but with one costing several times more than the other, it is likely that the more expensive one includes a comprehensive range of editing facilities, etc., whereas the cheaper one offers few extras. Some programs are better value than others, but as with most things in life, with computer software you generally get what you pay for.

Before buying any software you really need to look very carefully at its specification to check that it has the facilities that are of prime importance to you. Specification and features are not everything, and the user friendliness also needs to be taken into account. Really the only way of assessing this is to have the program demonstrated so that you can try it out for yourself. Even this is not a totally reliable way of assessing software. I have come across several programs that seemed to be the bees knees when I first started using them, but which with more experience seemed to be very slow and cumbersome to use. Conversely, I have encountered programs which seemed very slow and difficult to use at first, but which seemed very logical, fast, and easy to use after a couple of weeks regular use. With most of the more worthwhile programs a fair amount of learning effort will be required before you can fully exploit them.

Probably the greatest difficulty for the beginner is in understanding the functions of the main types of music software, and in deciphering all the software jargon which is used to describe their features. Hopefully, the descriptions in this chapter will clarify matters and will help you to find the pieces of software that are most likely to fulfil your requirements. Sorting out which of the likely contenders is the best choice for you is something you must organize yourself!

Sequencers

There can be little doubt that the most popular form of music software is the MIDI sequencer. There are two basic types of sequencer — real-time and step-time varieties. A real-time sequencer is one which records music played on a MIDI keyboard, and which is often used in place of multi-track tape recording. A step-time sequencer is one where music is manually entered into the computer in some way. This could be something as basic as typing in a list of notes and their durations, or it could be as sophisticated as a notation program where you put notes onto conventional staves using a mouse.

Here we will mainly be concerned with real-time sequencers. The reason for this is simply that these are by far the most popular type. In fact there are very few programs that only provide step-time sequencing. If you require a really good step-time sequencer it is usually a matter of looking for a real-time type which has very good editing facilities that can be used for easy step-time entry.

The right track
In order to qualify as a real-time sequencer a program needs to do no more than start recording MIDI data when a start key is depressed, finish recording when another key is depressed, and play back the sequence when a third key is operated. Commercial sequencing software goes well beyond this though, and even the cheaper sequencers offer multi-track capability. In other words, having recorded a sequence, you can go back to the beginning and record another track alongside that one. You can then go back to the beginning and record a third track, then a fourth track, and so on. Most sequencers permit at least sixteen tracks to be recorded, and sequencers which provide 32 or even 64 track recording are now available.

This multi-track facility is used in much the same way as multi-track tape recording. Tracks are laid down one by one, instrument by instrument, until a fully orchestrated piece is produced. There are major differences between the two methods though, with some definite advantages and a few drawbacks to the MIDI approach.

Taking the minus side first, the only really major drawback is that you need to have sufficient instruments with sufficient voices etc. in order to play back the completed piece properly. With multi-track tape recording you can use the same instrument for every track if necessary, setting it up for a new sound each time you move on to a fresh track. If a MIDI sequencer is used, you must be able to arrange the system so that each track will be played by an instrument or voice of an instrument that will provide the required sound. With modern instruments, which often offer something like multi-timbral operation on eight channels in mode 4 or multi mode, together with 16 to 32 note polyphony, finding something to give the right sound on each track is not as expensive as it once was.

There is a potential problem in that you could run out of MIDI channels. Being realistic about it, 16 channels with each one playing a different polyphonic instrument or voice of an instrument is probably more than most of us can handle anyway. If you should have big ideas though, they could outgrow MIDI's capabilities. On the other hand, some software and hardware permit the use of two or more independent MIDI outputs. The sequencer for the Atari ST that I use has an optional interface unit which fits onto the computer's serial port, and provides no less than three extra (and fully independent) MIDI outputs. This gives some sixty four channels, which should be sufficient for anyone (Figure 6.1).

Figure 6.1 The C-Lab Export interface for the ST computers. With the right software it gives a total of four separate MIDI outputs and 64 channels

On the plus side for MIDI, its main advantage must be the editing possibilities it provides. With a tape recording, speeding up or slowing down the tape in order to change the tempo of the music produces a corresponding increase or decrease in the pitch of the reproduced sound. Consequently, changing the speed of the tape is normally out of the question. With MIDI there is no problem of this type. The sequencer merely controls the rate at which the piece is played — the instruments determine the sounds and will not be affected by an increase or a decrease in the rate at which they are fed with data. It is quite in order to slow things down so that a difficult track can be played more easily, and to then speed everything up again once it has been recorded. If you simply do not like the tempo at which the piece was played, then it is quite possible to change it. You might even be able to change the replay rate of selected portions of the piece.

Remember that the recorded music exists only as a series of numbers that control note values, timing of events, the volume of notes, etc. If the sequencer has suitably comprehensive editing facilities it should be possible to change any item of data in order to get things just as you want them. An experienced tape editor can perform tasks such as grafting in the right note where the wrong one has been played, but this type of thing is much easier with a MIDI sequencer. A sequencer with good editing facilities should enable note values and durations to be changed with ease. You may even be able to do things such as alter velocity values, pitch bend data, etc.

As an example of an up-market editing feature which is available with some sequencers, global changes can be made to a specified type of MIDI data. Suppose that pitch bend data is giving too much

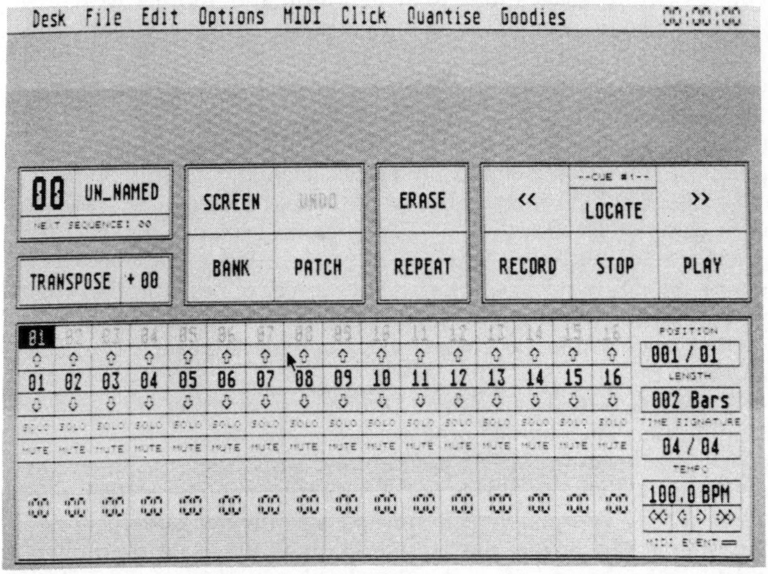

Figure 6.2 The Hollis Research Trackman sequencer start-up screen. Note the tape recorder style controls at the top right hand portion of the screen

113

or too little change in pitch. This could be due to the track being played badly, or due to the use of a different instrument to play the track. MIDI does not lay down any rules as to how much change in frequency a given pitch change value produces, and instruments differ significantly in this respect. Multiplying all pitch values by a certain value enables the degree of variation to be adjusted. A number greater than one gives increased pitch bend range — a value less than one gives decreased range.

Changing track

The ability to change data at the event level is a common feature on the more expensive sequencers, but it is only fair to point out that this type of editing is often very limited or totally absent on the cheaper ones. With the more basic sequencer programs most of the editing facilities are on a whole track basis, or can perhaps be applied to a selected part of a track. Of course, the up-market sequencers have this sort of thing in addition to event level editing rather than instead of it. Incidentally, the term 'event' is much used in sequencer specifications and advertising literature. An event is simply a MIDI message, but remember that each note requires two messages (one to switch it on and another to switch it off). If a sequencer has a storage capacity of 20000 events, this represents a maximum of 10000 notes (and less than this if other messages such as program changes and pitch bend are used).

Returning to the subject of track editing, it is usually possible to undertake such tasks as changing the MIDI channel, delete, copy, transpose, merge and time shift a track. Deleting is fairly obvious, and is used where a track has been played sufficiently badly to merit completely scrapping it. Copying and transposing are often used together. Suppose that you have recorded a track, and you require an identical track but an octave lower in pitch. Rather than playing and recording the track again but an octave lower, the original track could be copied and then transposed down one octave.

Merging two tracks into one is a useful ploy if you are running out of tracks. The obvious problem is that the two tracks will have to play on the same MIDI channel, and must therefore have the same sound. Actually, this is not strictly true, as some instruments can have two completely different sounds on the same channel. This operates by having one sound on notes above a certain pitch, and the other sound from the threshold note downwards. With suitable instruments it is therefore possible to have two sounds on

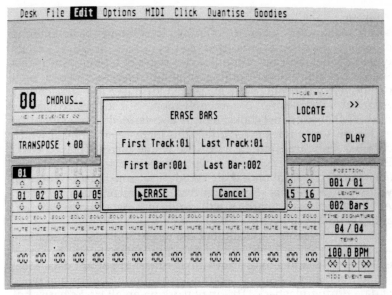

Figure 6.3 A pop-up menu in the Trackman sequencer. This one enables a selected part of the sequence to be erased

one track/MIDI channel, but only if their pitch ranges do not overlap.

Incidentally, some sequencers offer more tracks than there are MIDI channels. In some cases this is where the software supports multiple MIDI outputs, and each track can be assigned to a separate MIDI channel. In many cases the extra tracks can only be accommodated by using more than one track per MIDI channel. A 32 track sequencer of this type, on the face of it, does not offer any advantage over a 16 track type. I suppose that there is some possible advantage in having the extra tracks in that it might give greater editing capability. Once tracks have been merged it might not be possible to separate them again in order to permit individual editing.

Time shifting a track merely means moving it backwards or forwards in time relative to the other tracks. This would normally be used to make very minor adjustments to the relative timing of tracks in order to correct timing errors. It can also be used to purposely shift a track slightly out of synchronization with the others in order to make it stand out from them.

Filtering

Most sequencers seem to offer at least some basic filtering capability. In other words, they can be set up to ignore certain types of MIDI message. There are two types of filtering, since data can be ignored when recording so as to conserve memory, or it can be left out during transmission. Obviously not transmitting recorded data does not conserve memory, but it does reduce the risk of MIDI 'clog' or 'choke' as it is also termed. Remember that each time a new track is recorded, this increases the rate at which data has to be transmitted when the whole piece is played back. Each track might be perfectly acceptable on its own, but when they are all played back at once there could be too much data. With well written software this should not result in the computer crashing. At the very least though, it will result in a data queue forming, and the timing of events could be significantly altered.

Some of the more sophisticated sequencer software has routines which try to avoid this sort of thing by filtering out any non-essential data, and giving priority to the most important data. Most sequencers offer the simple alternative of filtering out certain types of data during playback. This may work on an all tracks basis, but ideally it would be possible to apply the filtering only to a selected track or tracks. The usual targets for this type of filtering are polyphonic aftertouch, channel aftertouch, pitch wheel change, and control change messages. Filtering of control messages is primarily aimed at eliminating modulation wheel changes. Using the modulation wheel, pitch wheel, or any type of aftertouch (but particularly the polyphonic type) tends to result in large quantities of MIDI data being generated.

Quantization

Quantization is a term which seems to pop up in a number of contexts, with slightly different meanings. In this context it refers to a timing correction facility. In theory, if your playing of a piece is a little ragged, using quantization tidies up the timing and makes it perfect. In reality things are not as simple as this. In the early days of sequencers the advertising copy writers tended to make quantization a big selling point. This was probably a case of making a virtue out of a necessity. Some of these early sequencers recorded the timing of notes with only quite poor resolution, and this resulted in notes being played back at a few standard lengths. This could make poorly played music sound much better, but it was just as likely to make a beautifully played piece sound rather

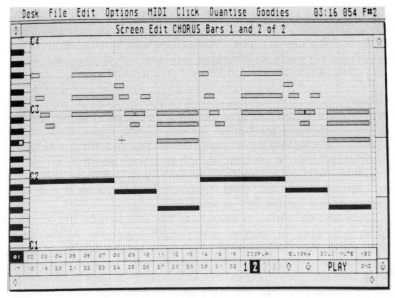

Figure 6.4 The grid editor of the Trackman. Note positions and lengths are easily changed by dragging the bars using the mouse and pointer

mechanical. Music is given expression in a number of ways, and subtle errors in the timing of notes is one of them.

Modern sequencers mostly record with excellent timing resolution, and do not have quantization out of necessity. Quantization techniques are often quite sophisticated, with several options available. As an example of modern quantization, one option might be to have note durations left unaltered, but to have the start positions of notes tidied up a little. Of course, quantization can only tidy up the timing to a limited degree, and if the timing of notes is a long way out there is no way in which the sequencer can know how long each one is supposed to be and where it should commence relative to the other notes. If you have a sequencer which can handle editing at MIDI event level, this probably represents a better way of correcting major errors. It could be quite time consuming to do so though. If a track requires playing skills beyond your capabilities there is always the option of step-time entry.

Quantization can either be carried out during the recording process, or during playback. Quantization while recording is less flexible, since it is irreversible. Recording a sequence into the computer, and then quantizing during playback is much more flexible. You can try out various types of quantization if the sequencer supports several types, and you can change your mind and cancel the quantization altogether if desired.

Groovy

While quantization can give technically very accurate sequences, it can also remove the human qualities of the reproduced music. Making quantization more sophisticated and providing a range of options reduces the problem, but does not eliminate it. The same problem exists with step-time sequences, where note durations and timing are usually very accurate. This tends to give a very expressionless 'music box' sound.

Some software tries to overcome this problem by introducing 'groove designs' or 'playing styles' into sequences. At the most basic level this just consists of a slight randomization of note durations and positions. This randomization is kept down to a level that prevents the music from simply sounding as though it has been badly played, but is made strong enough to eliminate or greatly reduce the music box effect.

The more sophisticated systems alter the timing of sequences in a regular manner that imposes a certain playing style on the reproduced music. This can operate using one of several preset patterns which is imposed on sequences to give playing styles, using what is a form of quantization. For example, a playing style might require the first half of each bar to be stretched slightly relative to the second half. Using the computer's mathematical capabilities it is not difficult to produce quantization that will give the desired effect. An alternative approach is to have the user play one track of a sequence, and to then use this as a template which is used when quantizing the other tracks. This is a very good system as it gives the required human feel to the music, but keeps all the tracks properly synchronized.

Of course, it is better if you can play all the tracks perfectly and forget quantization altogether. If you can not do so, then computers and MIDI help you to make the most of your talents. Your ideas no longer need to be limited by your playing ability.

Other features

One standard feature that I have not yet mentioned is the ability to 'dub' over a selected piece of a track. If you make a mistake, one way of correcting it is to use this dubbing facility. Another common feature is a built-in metronome. This may give the 'clicking' sounds via the computer's loudspeaker, or it may provide a so-called 'MIDI click' (or you might have the option of either). A MIDI click is simple a short high pitched note sent over one channel. Provided you provide a suitable instrument on this channel, the result is a sort of clicking sound which is a reasonable substitute for the normal metronome sound.

In the event

As pointed out previously, comprehensive event editing is a standard feature, but only on the more expensive sequencer programs. It is a very powerful feature, and one which usually more than justifies its extra cost.

Event editing can be carried out with the aid of a text only display, but most sequencers that make use of event editing have some form of graphics display, or a display that uses a combination of both text and graphics. Some of the more expensive sequencers offer two or three methods of event editing.

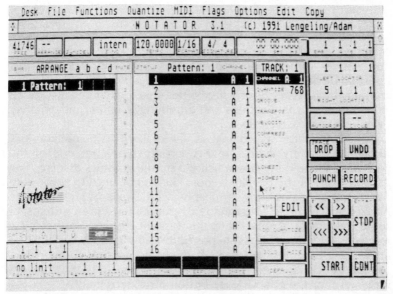

Figure 6.5 The C-Lab Notator start up screen. This is a sequencer of considerable power but it includes a comprehensive notation facility plus other types of editing

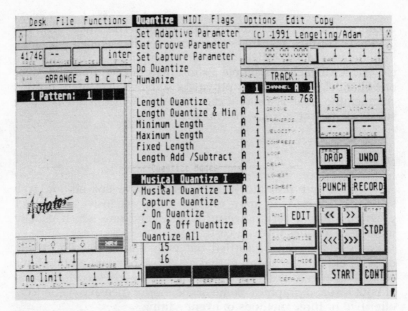

Figure 6.6 A Notator pop down menu. Menus can provide a large range of options and give access to further menus

A typical text only display would have one line per event, with each line including a description of the event type, timing values, note values (where appropriate), etc. Just how much of this information can be altered by the user varies from one program to another, but it would normally be possible to change such things as note values, the positions and durations of notes, and possibly even data such as velocity values.

An event editor which makes use of both text and graphics would be broadly similar to a text only type, but one of the parameters would be shown using a simple graphics display. The graphics part of the display is most likely to be used to show note durations and positions, probably with notes represented as horizontal bars on a background of vertical lines representing (say) some fraction of a note. With this type of display, control via a mouse is often possible. Note positions and durations can then be altered by 'dragging' the bars. It might be possible to alter data values by clicking on them with one mouse button for an increment, or the other mouse button for a decrement.

A graphics-only display might also be a notes-only display. In fact it will almost certainly display only note data. This type of

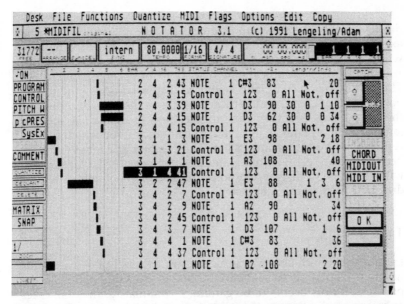

Figure 6.7 The main Notator edit screen. This shows all MIDI events and enables them to be edited

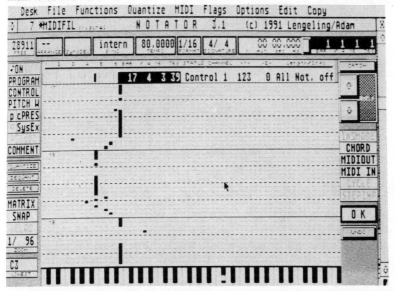

Figure 6.8 The piano roll type display of Notator. This program has an integrated approach that results in changes made using one editor being automatically reflected in the others

display could take the form of a grid having note values on one axis and time on the other. Notes would be represented as bars which could be dragged to vary their pitch, position, and duration. Another form of graphical note display is the 'player piano' type. This has an on-screen piano keyboard displayed across the top or bottom of the screen, and vertical bars above the keys to represent the notes. This is a very easy to use form of display as anyone familiar with a piano style keyboard can quickly see which note is represented by each graphics bar. The position and length of each bar shows the relative timing and positions of notes. Once again, with this type of display the notes can usually be manipulated by dragging them using a mouse

Take note

I suppose the ultimate in graphical event editors is a conventional notation display. Few sequencers have offered this option in the past, but it now seems to be gaining in popularity. In some cases only one track at a time can be displayed, but some sequencers now offer full score notation displays, which usually means the

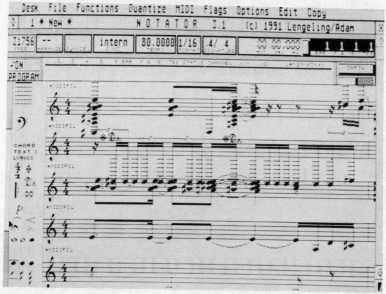

Figure 6.9 The notation editor of the C Lab Notator program. This is a sequence from another program which Notator has converted into standard notation form

ability to display up to 16 or 32 stave scores. This is perhaps a bit misleading, since the screen resolution is likely to impose a limit of about six or seven staves on the screen at any one time. Vertical scrolling enables the desired staves to be selected.

There are good reasons for the popularity of notation displays. One of these is that most musicians have been trained to use this form of musical notation. They naturally prefer this form of display to matrix style displays, etc. for most editing.

Another point in favour of the notation type of display is that it provides a lot of information per screenful. Conventional notation has evolved over hundreds of years, and has developed to the point where it would be difficult to devise a more compact means of storing music in paper and ink form (or monitor and pixel form). If you compare the amount of information displayed on the screen using a matrix piano type display with that of a notation display, the results are likely to be very revealing.

A notation display will probably provide something like three or four bars on up to about half a dozen tracks (i.e. up to about six staves). Matrix and player piano screens display about the same number of bars, but usually only shows one track at a time. Furthermore, the notation display does not merely provide note value and duration information, but also includes key signatures, dynamics information, written directions, etc. There is a weakness in a notation display in that it does not permit note values to be specified very precisely. For this reason it is very helpful to have some other form of editing display, such as a player piano type, so that any necessary fine tuning of note lengths can be undertaken.

Rest and play
Another point in favour of having a conventional notation display is that it is usually accompanied by a printout facility. The capability of producing neatly printed out scores for your master-pieces is clearly a great asset. With an integrated sequencer/notation program you can play compositions on the keyboard, track by track if necessary, and then have the notation part of the program display the piece in conventional notation form, and print it out if required.

This is slightly idealising things, and in reality some editing of the notation display will probably be needed in order to get things just right. A common problem is that of notes being displayed as of very short duration with a lot of rests padding out the spaces between them. The problem here is that the programs take the length of a note to be equal to the duration that the key was pressed. In other words, the length between the note on and note off messages. This may seem reasonable, but remember that many instrument sounds do not finish as soon as the key is released. Piano and guitar sounds for example, can sustain for several seconds after the key has been released. With these sounds the duration between the MIDI note on and note off messages may be substantially shorter than the true duration of the note.

Some programs offer a way around this problem, which is basically to extend note values to fill in the gaps, rather than adding in lots of rests. This may not always give the desired result. It is up to the user to select the method which gives the best result, and to undertake any manual editing that might be needed in order to get things just right. Although these programs are sometimes put forward as being ideal for someone who has not had any training in conventional notation, this is perhaps not entirely true. Someone who is reasonably expert in notation stands a much better chance of producing note-perfect printouts.

It is only fair to point out that while most sequencer programs which have a notation section can convert recorded sequences into music displayed in conventional notation form, the reverse operation of converting a notation display into MIDI messages that can be used to play the piece via MIDI is not always possible. You need to be careful to select a suitable program if you will want to do a lot of step-time sequencing using the notation section of a sequencer. If you are familiar with conventional music notation, probably the easiest method of undertaking step-time sequencing is to use a notation program, and to then do some fine tuning using something like a matrix type event editor in order to get things just right. If you are not cognisant with conventional notation, a program which has a good matrix or player-piano type editor will probably represent the best option.

There are some programs which are primarily intended for producing printed out scores. Appropriately enough, these are called 'notation' or 'score writer' programs. These do not usually have any real-time sequencing capability, or if they do it is likely to be of a very limited nature. In some cases they do not even have the ability to act as step-time sequencers, and are effectively note processors for producing sheet music. The importance of MIDI these days is such that most score writer programs do now have the ability to output pieces over MIDI. In fact some programs of this type have quite sophisticated MIDI data editing facilities which are comparable to those found on the better real-time sequencers.

If you are only interested in step-time sequencing and printing out scores, this type of program would seem to be a good choice.

Integration

For the ultimate in versatility an integrated approach to MIDI data handling is required. In other words, a program that provides real-time sequencing together with various ways of displaying data, including a sophisticated multi-stave notation facility. The text and graphics displays are produced largely from the recorded MIDI data, and enable the MIDI data to be edited at event level. This permits step-time sequencing with several means of entering data, including the placing of notes onto the staves in the notation part of the program. As all the data displays are produced largely from the MIDI data in memory; changing a piece of data using one editing method will result in any necessary changes to the other displays being made automatically. Music entered by real-time sequencing can be displayed in notation form and printed out if desired. Music entered into the notation part of the program, or one of the other editing systems, can be played over MIDI if desired.

'Do everything' programs of this type enable you to do pretty well anything you like, but are inevitably very complex pieces of software. Integrated programs of this type are noticeably thin on the ground at present, but this seems likely to be the way of things to come. Due to their complexity though, they seem unlikely to be available at the budget end of the market in the foreseeable future, and really comprehensive programs of this type are not likely to be available for eight bit computers. Presumably these techniques could be applied to good effect on eight bit software though, albeit with some of the bells and whistles omitted, the maximum sequence size more limited, and the operating speed that much less.

In practice

Obviously the precise method of using a sequencer depends on the particular program used, and the method of note entry. However, we can cover the basics of using a sequencer provided things are viewed in suitably broad terms. For specific details you must carefully study the manual for whichever piece of software you choose. Computer and software manuals are not noted for being particularly easy to follow, and some determined effort may be required!

If we take real-time sequencing first, having managed to get everything wired up and ready to go, the first task is to name the first track. This may seem trivial, but it is an important operation. You should ideally be able to use quite long track names so that you can make it perfectly clear what sound should be produced by the MIDI channel for each track (e.g. Casio CZ1 Trumpet 2). At the time you produce the piece this might all be clear in your mind, but what if you return to it six months or more later?

Virtually all sequencers provide some sort of countdown facility so that you do not need to operate the start control with your big-toe and then start playing at once! Virtually all sequencers provide a metronome facility, which can be important with some types of sequencing. The countdown facility will work in conjunction with this.

The main controls of sequencers almost invariably take the form of pseudo tape recorder controls. This makes them very easy to use, as presumably most people will not need any long explanations of on-screen controls marked start, stop, fast-forward, etc. The fast-forward and reverse controls might work exactly like their tape recorder counterparts, moving rapidly backwards and forwards through the sequence. They might simply provide a means of jumping instantly to the beginning or end of the sequence though, or you might have the luxury of both types of control. In order to help you navigate your way through sequences there should be an on-screen tape counter. Like the real thing, this might be scaled arbitrarily, or it might be scaled in minutes and seconds (or bars and notes). Like any built-in metronome, this will work in conjunction with the countdown facility.

Having started the sequencer, played a track, and stopped the recording, you can then replay it to see if it is up to scratch. If not, you can delete the track and try again, attempt to over-dub the unsatisfactory section or sections, or if there is an event editor, try editing the MIDI data in order to improve matters. It is more than a little helpful if the sequencer has an 'undo' facility. This simply reverses the last operation so that if you should make a mistake when editing, or should simply change your mind, you can quickly put things back the way they were. Where such a facility is lacking it is a good idea to regularly save the piece to tape or disk. If necessary, you can then go back to the last backup on disk/tape and try again. It is a good idea to take regular backups anyway. Remember that in the event of a power loss or computer fault, anything in memory (which includes your masterpiece) will be lost.

If the piece is only a single track type, then once you have done any necessary editing the sequence is finished. If multi-tracking is to be used, it is time to move onto the next track. You must switch to the next track using the appropriate control, so that you do not record the new track on top of (and in place of) the first one. Most sequencers have warning messages and will not do this type of thing unless you confirm that this is definitely what you want to do. The new track is then named, and you may wish to select a new MIDI channel for it at this stage. This is not usually essential, since you can normally change the channel of a track as often as you like after it has been recorded. It is therefore quite in order to record everything on channel 1, and to assign channels later, although this is not necessarily a good method of working. It should be possible to hear existing tracks playing while a new one is added, but obviously the existing tracks must be on the right channels for this to work properly. Having recorded the second track, the piece is then replayed to determine how good (or otherwise) it sounds, and any necessary editing or dubbing is carried out. Having added a second track, you might find a previously unnoticed problem with the first track. You can then switch back to track one and carry out any necessary editing.

This process is continued track-by-track until you have built up the complete piece. Any appropriate track editing facilities can be used to speed up the process, such as copying and transposing one track to produce another. Where repeat sections are needed it will probably be possible to copy a section of track and graft it in at the appropriate place. Some sequencers even let you copy sections from one track to another. After a final play-through and any last minute editing, your masterpiece is finished.

Step-time sequencing is inevitably going to be a much more laborious process. This is presumably why it is less popular than real-time sequencing. Methods of note entry vary greatly from one sequencer to another. You may have to type in note values and lengths, or at the other extreme it may simply be a matter of using the mouse or keyboard to place notes onto the on-screen staves. The notation method of note entry is the one which most people find the most tolerable. If you intend to do a lot of step-time sequencing and your knowledge of notation is not all it could be, a little studying of the subject would probably be time well spent.

With some programs the MIDI data will be affected by such things as dynamics markings on the score. With others these are treated as 'ornaments' which have no effect on the MIDI data. In either case you are unlikely to be completely satisfied with results unless there is some means of editing MIDI data in order to fine tune things to your liking. Like real-time sequencing, you can usually assign each track to a MIDI channel any time you like, and reassign channels when and as often as you like.

Voice editors

While sequencers of various types account for a sizeable percentage of music software sales, they are by no means the only type of music program available. Probably the next most popular form of music software are the voice editors. In the days when analogue synthesizers ruled supreme this type of thing was unnecessary. Synthesizers had rows of front panel mounted knobs and switches, and any desired part of the sound generator circuit could be adjusted almost instantly. You just grabbed the right knob and started twiddling!

Figure 6.10 The Yamaha TG100 expander unit has 192 on-board sounds, but also acts as a MIDI interface for a PC or Mac computer

This method of control became impracticable as instruments increased in sophistication. The number of adjustable parameters steadily grew, and as multi-timbral instruments came along, the number of parameters was multiplied by the number of voices offered by these instruments. The number of adjustable parameters could be (literally) into the hundreds. At first the normal way around the problem was to have a set of push button switches, an LCD or LED display, and just one control knob. You keyed in the number of the parameter you wished to adjust, checked on the display that you had selected the right one, and then adjusted it using the control knob.

This system worked very well, and was a good compromise between cost and ease of use. Exactly why manufacturers decided to drop this method I do not know, but it seems to be little used these days. Most instruments now use a similar method, but with the control knob replaced by two push buttons, one to increase the parameter value, and the other to decrease it. The display shows the parameter value. Making adjustments using this method tends to be quite slow and laborious. This system is popular with the equipment producers because it is cheap and easy to implement,

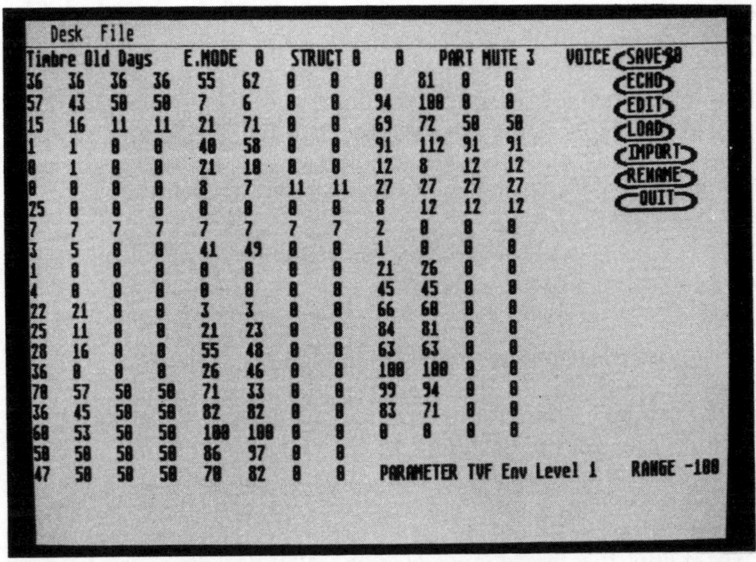

Figure 6.11 A simple but effective voice editor for the D110 running on an ST computer. This type of software can greatly simplify setting up your own sounds.

but it is loathed by most users. Most people have simply given up trying to program their own sounds and have settled for using the factory preset sounds. Most instruments are supplied with a large number of preset sounds, often with others available on plug-in ROM cartridges. Sales of modern synthesizers are probably very dependent on a good range of preset sounds being available.

One way of getting improved control over the sound generator circuits of a syntheziser is to obtain one of the programmer units that are available for some instruments. These have banks of switches and control knobs which makes programming sounds very much quicker and easier. As virtually all MIDI equipped instruments provide control of the sound generator circuits by way of MIDI, another alternative is to have a program which mimics an add-on controller unit. The same control knobs and switches are present, but in the form of on-screen representations that can be manipulated using the mouse.

There are other ways of implementing voice editing software, and at a basic level there can be a collection of parameter values on the screen. These can be incremented or decremented, as desired, using the keyboard or possibly using a mouse. An up-market approach to adjusting some parameters is to use the graphics capability of the computer. For example, if the envelope shape of a voice is to be adjusted, rather than having on-screen representations of the envelope controls there could be a graph showing the envelope shape. The graph could then be dragged into the desired shape using the mouse, with the program working out the envelope values to give the selected shape and sending them over MIDI. Usually any changes you make are rapidly sent to the instrument so that you can hear the results of changes as you make them.

Librarians

If you undertake a lot of programming your own sounds you will soon accumulate a large number of sounds. Only a limited number can be stored within the instrument's internal memory, and in order to store your own sounds in this way you will probably have to sacrifice some or all of the factory preset sounds. Most modern synthesizers seem to offer some form of external data storage, such as cassette tapes, RAM cartridges, or (very rarely) computer disks. Instruments that are equipped with MIDI usually have another option, which is to load and save data via MIDI.

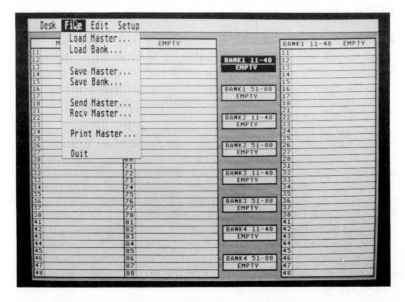

Figure 6.12 The Worx-4-Me librarian program showing a pop-down menu. At this stage no data has been loaded into the program

Librarian software tends to be confused with voice editing software, which is understandable because many voice editing programs include a librarian facility. In other words, sounds can be loaded from the instrument into the computer, and then saved to disk via the computer's disk drive. They can then be retrieved from disk and loaded from the computer to the instrument when they are needed. As dumps of voice data do not usually involve large amounts of data, and the capacity of most disk drives is a few hundred kilobytes or more, this is a very economic means of saving sound data. Each disk may well be able to store over one hundred sets of sound data, and will probably cost only about one pound.

It is also a convenient way of handling things in that the computer can provide help in tracking down the sounds you require. Ideally this help would be in the form of comprehensive database facilities, but librarian software varies considerably in the sophistication of the database facilities provided.

Visual editors

At one time if you wanted an instrument that would provide a really varied selection of sounds there was little choice but to opt for a synthesizer. However, in recent years, samplers have become very much more sophisticated and have massively dropped in price. They have become very popular — possibly even more popular than synthesizers.

Sampling a sound is very easy with most of these instruments, but getting really good results from a sample is often far from easy. Much sampling consists of recording a short piece of sound and then looping it in order to obtain a sound that is as long as desired. The shortness of the recorded sound can be due to the memory restrictions of the sampler, or only a short version of the sound being available. In either case, repeating the end part of the signal over and over again enables the sound to be continued indefinitely. This sounds simple enough, but human hearing is very good at detecting inaccuracies in sounds. For looping to work well it is essential for the looped part of the signal to be a number of whole cycles.

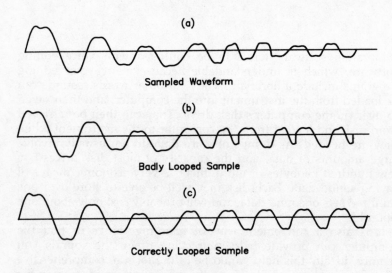

Figure 6.13 Looping of sampled waveforms

Figure 6.13 helps to explain the problem In Figure 6.13(a) we have the waveform of the recorded signal, and in Figure 6.13(b) there is a badly looped version of the signal. This sustains indefinitely in the required manner, but the waveform does not bear that much resemblance to the original. When dealing with sample waveforms you always need to keep in mind that waveforms tend to look a great deal better than they sound! The waveform of Figure 6.13(b) would probably just give a terrible buzzing sound at completely the wrong pitch. The waveform of Figure 6.13(c) is much more expertly looped, and would be much more likely to give good results.

If you have a sampler which is equipped with a good graphics display it is not too difficult to pick out looping points that are likely to give good results. A certain amount of experimentation is likely to be needed in order to get things just right, but with the aid of a waveform display you can almost instantly home in on looping points that are likely to need no more than some fine tuning. Without a waveform display to guide you, things are very hit-and-miss. You have to pick a loop point at random, and then use trial and error to find a loop point that matches it well. If a really quiet match can not be found for the initial loop point, another has to be selected, and the process repeated. This procedure is repeated as many times as is necessary in order to find really good loop points, or until you give up in frustration!

Many of the current samplers seem to be equipped with some form of built-in waveform display, or have a socket for a monitor. Not all are equipped with a graphics display though, and some that are only have a fairly low resolution type. These samplers can benefit from the use of a visual editor program which loads samples via MIDI, and then provides a graphics display of the waveform to aid loop point editing. In most cases these programs are quite sophisticated. You can usually view the waveform of a complete sample, zoom in on one section of a sample, or possibly even zoom in on two parts of the waveform which will be displayed in separate windows. This zooming ability is important because most samples have hundreds of cycles, and in order to give good results have to be looped over a few dozen cycles.

Visual editor programs are not particularly cheap, but can be very worthwhile for someone who is going to produce a lot of their own sound samples. However, if a few sets of factory disks will fulfil your requirements, they might actually be cheaper and will save a lot of time.

Other types

This covers the main categories of music software, but there are a number of other types available. There are a number of educational programs available if you want to brush up on your music theory. A computer, especially used in conjunction with MIDI and a suitable instrument, is ideal for educational purposes. Even a lot of non-educational music software is likely to teach you a great deal and take you to a level that you might have previously thought impossible. The only real problem with much of the music education software is that it is priced on the basis of being used year after year in educational establishment. This makes it a bit expensive for one-off personal use.

An interesting form of music software is one which effectively turns a sound sampler into a synthesizer. The basic idea is for the user to adjust on-screen synthesizer controls (Figure 6.14), and for the computer to then work out the correct sample values for these settings and send them to the sampler. This is certainly an attractive type of software for the sampler user, and one which has tremendous potential. The main problem is that with present

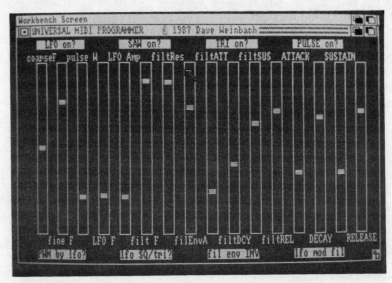

Figure 6.14 A control panel program running on the Amiga. The mouse and pointer are used to control the 'sliders' and 'switches' (David Weinbach)

microcomputer technology the process of working out the sampler values, even for the more easily modelled synthesizers, takes quite a long time. It can take hours in fact! You therefore need to have a pretty accurate idea of the control settings needed to produce the required sound, as numerous fine adjustments to get things just right would take an inordinate amount of time.

There are various other programs available, including librarians for system exclusive messages, and so-called intelligent programs that can aid with harmonization. Obviously some of the programs that are outside the mainstream music categories are of strictly limited appeal. On the other hand, it can be worthwhile looking through some music software catalogues and studying the descriptions of the more unusual programs. You might just stumble across something that would be of tremendous benefit to you.

PD and shareware

Music software is not the cheapest type available, and even the least expensive of these programmes seem to be several times the price of the average games program. This is a common cause of complaint amongst the electronic music fraternity, but the prices charged are not unreasonable. It takes a great deal of programming time in order to produce most music software, and there is no real potential for mass sales on the same scale as less specialized programs such as games and word processors. The programming costs, plus those of production, distribution, and advertising, therefore have to be borne by a relatively small number of users. Really cheap commercial music software is probably not a practical proposition.

Although normal commercial music software is unlikely to be available at rock-bottom prices, there is an alternative in the form of 'PD' (public domain) software. This type of software is actually three distinctly different types, which are PD, shareware, and commercial demonstration programs. This third category is a potentially useful one for the budding computer musician. These programs give you the opportunity to try out full price commercial software and thoroughly evaluate it. All you pay is a few pounds for the disks. If you discover that the software is not what you want, or you find it difficult to use, you have not wasted large sums of money. If you like the programs, then you can buy the full price versions.

Obviously the demonstration versions are not fully operational, and they are supplied with little or no documentation. The programs are usually 'crippled' by disabling the routines that handle the saving of data to disk. With a demonstration sequencer you might be able to produce sequences as long and complex as you like, but after switching off the computer your work is lost for ever. Another software crippling technique is to have the program fully operational, but to limit the amount of memory that can be used for data storage. This enables the program to be used normally, but with a sequencer for example, you would be limited to quite short sequences. The least helpful type of demonstration is the 'running' type. These simply go through the basics of operating the program, with the program operating itself and supplying you with on-screen notes to explain what it is doing. You have no opportunity to operate the program yourself (although you can break into some running demonstration programs and try them out). Demonstration software is a very good idea, but as yet there are no demonstration versions of most music programs.

Shareware programs are a form of commercial software, but they are distributed by companies that only charge for the cost of the disk plus a modest fee to cover copying fees, overheads, etc. They are also distributed by other means, and you are at liberty to copy and distribute these programs to your friends. Of course, this is illegal with normal commercial software, and some programs are copy protected so that copies can not be made using ordinary copying techniques, or copies can be made in the normal way but will not work properly.

The idea of shareware is that if you do not like the program, you pay nothing more, and have wasted very little money. If you do like the program, then the appropriate registration fee should be sent to its author. The manuals for this type of program are normally in the form of a text file on the disk, which you read via the computer, or print out on paper. Registration often brings a proper manual, plus possibly other benefits as well (the latest version of the program for example). The only thing that stops you from using the program and not sending in the registration fee is your conscience!

There is a vast amount of shareware available for most of the popular computers, but only a very small proportion of this is music software. Nevertheless, it might be worthwhile looking through some PD software catalogues to see what you can find. You do not have a lot to lose. On the other hand, be warned that a lot of shareware software has not been fully debugged, and tends to crash quite frequently. The documentation is usually very sparse, and it can take a lot of effort to learn how to use these programs.

Explanations of exactly what constitutes PD software vary somewhat. My understanding of the term 'public domain' is that it applies to anything (music, books, software, etc.) where no one holds the copyright. In most cases this is due to work falling out of copyright due to its age. In a computer software context a more likely cause is that the originator of the work has decided not to claim copyright on it. The program is then free for anyone to use, copy, distribute and modify.

While there is a great deal of true PD software around, it mostly consists of short programs and few major works, which is understandable. Many of these programs are quite trivial, and, quite frankly, many of them do not work at all well. There are some good PD programs available though, including a few music orientated types. Once again, it might be worthwhile looking through a few PD catalogues to see if you can find anything of interest. Do not set your hopes too high though.

7 MIDI instruments

In many respects the requirements for electronic music instruments are much the same, whether or not they will be used as part of a computer music system. For most users the quality of the sounds will be of foremost importance, and quite rightly so. Few people have unlimited budgets, and obviously the cost of instruments is another important factor. On the other hand, there are other factors which are very important for units that will be used in a computer based system, and which must be taken into account when choosing your instruments. Taking an extreme example, an instrument which sounds great and costs very little is not much use in a computer setup if it has no means of control other than the keyboard. To be of any use in a computer music context an instrument must have some form of external control, and it should ideally have a very full MIDI implementation, plus plenty of voices etc.

Taking a less extreme example, a bargain instrument which only provides mode 1 and mode 3 operation with no multi-timbral operation possible might be of limited use, and not such a bargain after all. On the other hand, an instrument that provides something like 32 note polyphony with eight or 16 voice multi-timbral operation, could be all you will need. The capabilities of instruments under computer control must be carefully weighed-up, especially if you will only have one or two instruments in the system. The fact that two instruments have MIDI interfaces does not mean that their sequencing possibilities are the same. One could be stretching MIDI to the limit while the other might offer only the most basic form of control via its MIDI ports. You should carefully delve into the MIDI specifications of instruments before buying anything.

138

The interface

The instruments in a computer based system do not necessarily need to have a MIDI interface. Instruments having gate/CV interfaces can be computer controlled. Although they are not produced any more, instruments of this type are available at quite low secondhand prices. The sounds of many synthesizers of the gate/CV era are superb, and are preferred by some to the sounds of modern instruments.

Despite this, they are not a particularly attractive proposition for the modern computer musician. Using this method of interfacing you have to contend with the problems of standardization (or the lack of it) associated with the pre-MIDI era. You also have to contend with the severe limitations of this form of interfacing. Probably worst of all, these days you will find it difficult to find computer interfaces and software that will work with instruments of this type.

At the other end of the price range there are some instruments which operate using a standard computer serial interface of the RS232C or RS422 types. However, we are talking in terms of very expensive software and hardware which is not a practical proposition for most of us. This type of thing is strictly for the dedicated and successful professional musician.

Up to spec

MIDI is not the only choice, but for the majority of us it would seem to represent the only practical one. Modern MIDI equipped instruments have some quite impressive specifications, mostly offer good value for money, produce a wide range of superb sounds, and with few exceptions have quite full MIDI specifications. The competition is so fierce that any instrument which has a serious deficiency is unlikely to stay on sale for very long!

It is important when you are selecting instruments that you do not jump to any conclusions about the MIDI specification. Modern MIDI equipped instruments almost invariably have good MIDI implementations, but most instruments lack at least one or two features though. MIDI is a set of standards that enables a wide range of features to be implemented, but not all of them are necessarily supported by any given instrument. Obviously features can only be implemented if an instrument's hardware supports them, and with budget instruments there are likely to be several gaps in the specification. If a particular feature is of special importance to you, carefully check the specifications of the instruments on your short-list to see if they support it. If you do not see a feature mentioned in an instrument's specification, it is probably safe to assume that it does not have it.

Any instrument should support note on and note off messages, plus a range of other basic messages types such as pitch bend, program change, mode change, and certain control messages (particularly modulation depth and sustain pedal on/off). At one time relatively few instruments were touch sensitive, and most transmitted dummy velocity bytes in note on and note off messages. These instruments simply ignored the velocity information on received note messages.

The present situation is very different though, and there are very few new MIDI equipped instruments currently on sale which do not implement touch sensitivity. With all the instruments I have encountered, only note on messages are transmitted with proper velocity information. A dummy value of 0 is sent in note off messages, and many instruments seem to use note on values with a velocity value of 0 for switching off notes (something that is permitted by the MIDI specification). Similarly, velocity data bytes in received note off messages are just ignored. This does not really matter, since the normal use of velocity information is to control the volume of notes, plus possibly the instrument's filtering. There is no obvious role for note off velocity information, although I suppose that it could be used to control something like the release phase of an ADSR envelope shaper. This would seem to be a far from essential feature though.

In touch

Any form of pressure sensitivity (aftertouch) used to be extremely rare indeed. The polyphonic version still is, but is to be found on a few instruments. Channel aftertouch is more common, and is adequate for many purposes. If you are sequencing a number of monophonic channels using mode 4, then channel aftertouch would seem to be all that is needed. It is only when there is more than one note per channel that polyphonic aftertouch gives more control. Aftertouch is used to control the volume of notes after the initial phase of the envelope (which is controlled by the velocity data). I suppose that it would be possible to have an instrument that implemented aftertouch but which was not velocity sensitive.

In practice, an instrument which has any form of aftertouch invariably implements velocity sensitivity (but one which is velocity sensitive does not necessarily implement any form of aftertouch).

Aftertouch is important for accurately synthesizing many instruments, as without the control over the instrument's dynamics that aftertouch provides, it is impossible to mimic the playing styles of many instruments. A lot of the expression in music played on strings and wind instruments for instance, is provided by subtle changes in the dynamics. Even if you are only interested in purely 'electronic' sounds and are not interested in synthesizing acoustic instrument sounds, aftertouch still provides that much more control over the music, and is a real asset.

The right modes

MIDI modes are important to most sequencing work. Omni modes (1 and 2) are not much use for most sequencing, since there is no ability to direct each track to a different instrument or voice of an instrument. If you only wish to sequence a single (non-multitimbral) instrument, such as an electronic organ or piano, then I suppose that mode 1 will suffice. This is largely ignoring the power and versatility of MIDI though. Most people who use sequencers require the added potency of modes 3 and 4. Several instruments operating in mode 3 is nice if you can afford it, but for most of us mode 4 or a combination of modes 3 and 4 are more practical propositions.

Mode 4 can sometimes provide disappointing results, even though on the face of it each channel assigned to mode 4 operation only needs to play one note at a time. Results can sometimes sound rather muted, and not as expected. The point to bear in mind here is that what appears to be a monophonic channel when you look at the score, might actually have several notes sounding at once. This is due to the fact that on some instruments, playing one note does not necessarily result in the previous one being cut off abruptly. With an instrument such as a woodwind type, or an accurate synthesis of such an instrument, obviously there is genuinely only one note at a tine playing. With instruments such as pianos and harps, matters are much less clear cut. How abruptly (or otherwise) notes are cut off depends to some extent on how the instrument is played and on the note range in question, but the release phase is often of significant duration. It is for this reason that electronic pianos are often sixteen (or more) note polyphonic, and that a polyphonic instrument is sometimes needed in order to play what appears to be a monophonic track.

Even having most tracks occupied by mode 4 instruments, with those requiring polyphonic operation taken up by mode 3 instruments, it can still take a lot of expensive hardware to provide something that will do full justice to every track of a sequence. This is where some form of multi mode really comes into its own. Even with something like an eight note polyphonic instrument, a flexible multi mode can greatly enhance the usefulness of an instrument. With an instrument such as a 32 note polyphonic type, a fairly crude form of multi mode is sufficient to give some really good results. In fact a single instrument of this type, capable of something like eight note multi-timbral operation, can provide some really good results even without the aid of other instruments. The built-in demo pieces of some Roland instruments show just how impressive results can be using a modern multi-timbral instrument.

For sequencing work some form of multi mode is a tremendous advantage, and many users are prepared to compromise slightly in other departments in order to get an instrument which supports this feature. Fortunately, most modern MIDI instruments seem to offer a multi mode, and there should be no difficulty in finding an instrument which has this mode plus the other features that are important to you.

Pre-used

Modern electronic music instruments offer outstanding value for money, and good secondhand equipment offers what is usually even better value for money. However, you do need to proceed with caution. Apart from the usual potential problems of buying secondhand, you need to bear in mind that MIDI is a relatively recent development. It largely came into being during 1981, but it did not really see the light of day until 1982. Even then it was not really what could be termed an over-night success. In the early days, MIDI was to be found on few instruments, and for several years after its inception many instruments had what could only be regarded as a rather crude MIDI implementation. As the years went by, some instruments which at their launch did not have MIDI ports, suddenly gained them, while other instruments which originally had a sparse implementation of MIDI gradually gained much more full versions.

This raises a degree of uncertainty for the secondhand buyer, who needs to check carefully that he or she is getting the right version of an instrument. The fact that the current version of an instrument has certain MIDI features does not necessarily mean that earlier versions of the instrument will have all of those features. It is worth bearing in mind that upgrades are sometimes available for early versions of instruments, bringing them up to the full current standard. This often involves nothing more than the changing of one or two ROM chips. When the MIDI specification of an instrument is improved, it often involves changes in the software with no hardware changes at all. Incidentally, you may sometimes encounter the term 'firmware'. This is software that is contained on a ROM chip, and which is therefore a mixture of hardware and software. Computing is well known for its quaint terminology!

Implementation charts

The key to discovering the MIDI capabilities of any instrument, be it new or secondhand, is the MIDI implementation chart. These are a feature of all the manuals for MIDI equipped instruments that I have encountered. Unfortunately, this information does not usually seem to be included in advertising literature for instruments. You may therefore need to press manufacturers, agents, or retailers in order to obtain these charts. It is well worthwhile doing so though, as with the aid of a MIDI implementation chart you can quickly and accurately assess the MIDI capabilities of an instrument.

A MIDI implementation chart is basically just a list of MIDI message types, with some form of indication to show whether or not each of these message types is implemented. In most cases transmitted and received data are detailed separately, as some types of message or data may be transmitted but not recognised (or vice versa). For example, a MIDI expander will recognise note on and note off messages, but with no keyboard it is obviously incapable of transmitting either of these.

When looking at MIDI implementation charts you should read the small print. There are often some brief explanatory notes at the end of the chart which detail any special limitations or additions to the instrument's MIDI implementation. As a couple of examples, it might be possible to enable or disable certain MIDI features via front panel controls, or you might find that a feature such as pitch bend affects all voices when an instrument is in mode 4, regardless of which channel/voice this information is directed at. The example MIDI implementation chart provided below should give you a good idea of what to expect. Provided you understand the main MIDI message types, interpreting one of these charts is not difficult.

Function	Transmitted	Recognised	Remarks
Note on	O	O	Note = 12 to 108 velocity = 0 to 127
Note off	X	X	Note on with V= 0 used
Pitch bend	O	O	
Prog change	O	O	0 to 63
Poly aftertouch	X	X	
Chan aftertouch	O	O	
Cont change 1	O	O	Mod wheel
Cont change 2 – 6	X	X	
Cont change 7	O	O	Master volume
Cont change 8 – 63	X	X	
Cont change 64	X	O	Sustain pedal
Cont change 65 – 120	X	X	
Cont change 121	X	O	Reset controls
Mode	O	O	
Sys exclusive	O	O	
Aux message	X	O	Local on/off
Aux message	X	O	All notes off
Aux message	X	O	Active sensing
Aux message	X	X	Reset
Sys common	X	X	
Sys real-time	X	X	

Notes
O = feature implemented. X = feature not implemented. Only modes 1, 3, and 4 are implemented.

Results

When you first start using a computer for sequencing, and you have mastered the basic techniques of using the software, it can all seem to be very easy. You record tracks or use step-time entry, and you make sure that there is a suitable instrument or voice of an instrument on each track. If you are only intending to use 'electronic' sounds, then I suppose that things really are this simple. If you use 'real' instrument sounds, things can be a little more difficult. The nature of the sound produced by most acoustic instruments changes significantly over their compass, and the sound might also change dramatically depending on how loudly or softly the instrument is played. There may also be different ways of playing an instrument, such as bowed or plucked strings.

Many modern instruments try to accommodate these changes in timbre. At a basic level the use of program changes may be useful, especially where two different playing methods and two totally different sounds must be accommodated on a track. At a more sophisticated level, some instruments can have different sounds using a keyboard split technique. High pitched notes can have a different sound to low pitched ones, or a multi-way split might be possible. This makes it possible to mimic the changes in timbre that occur over the range of notes covered by an instrument. A similar split point technique can be utilized with MIDI velocity values, so that high volume sounds have a different timbre to quiet ones. This can even be used to handle something like the sound of an over-blown wind instrument. With some instruments both types of split point technique can be used simultaneously. Velocity sensitive instruments usually permit the velocity value to control the filtering, and this is a simple but effective way of giving a different sound depending on how loudly an instrument is played.

Provided you have enough instruments, they have good specifications, and you are prepared to take the time to fully exploit their features, some really excellent results can be obtained. With the help of MIDI and a computer, many musicians find that they are soon producing music of a quality and complexity that they would never have been able to produce in any other way. This is something you should certainly bear in mind when putting a system together. What might seem like an adequate number of tracks etc. when you first set up a system can seem to be a bit limiting once you start to get the hang of things, and your ideas start to blossom. Funds permitting, it is a good idea to build up a system that goes some way beyond your immediate needs. You will probably soon progress to the point where you can fully exploit the equipment. Be patient when learning to use a new computer music system. You will be doing things in a way that is unlikely to have much in common with the way you have worked before. It is only reasonable to expect the 'fish out of water' feeling at first, with a lot of mistakes and doubts about the whole idea! With a little perseverance you should soon find that you can use the system intuitively, and will wonder how you ever managed to do things any other way.

Appendix 1
Glossary of terms

Active sensing
Not many MIDI devices seem to implement this feature. The basic idea is for a MIDI active sensing message to be periodically sent by the MIDI controller. If a broken cable or something of this nature results in a breakdown in communications, the controlled equipment will detect the absence of the active sensing messages, and will switch off all notes. Otherwise, any notes that are left switched on will remain so indefinitely.

ADSR
The standard form of envelope shaper. Its adjustable parameters are attack rate (A), decay rate (D), sustain level (S), and release rate (R). Some older synthesizers have a more simple attack/decay envelope shaper, but most modern instruments have more complex mutli-stage types (like the eight stage Casio envelope generators).

Aftertouch
Some electronic musical instruments respond to the pressure applied to keys. The key pressure normally controls the volume of the note, and possibly affects the filtering as well. Channel aftertouch is a simplified form where all the notes on a MIDI channel have the same volume, which is a sort of average key pressure for those notes. Polyphonic aftertouch is the full implementation where each note can have different volume level.

Analogue to digital converter
Many electronic musical instruments have largely digital circuits, but the 'real-world' deals in analogue quantities. The purpose of an analogue to digital converter is to take in 'real' signals and convert them into a form that digital circuits can deal with. For

example, a converter of this type is needed in a sound sampler in order to change the varying voltage from the microphone into a form that is suitable for storage in the instrument's digital memory circuits. A digital to analogue converter is used to convert digital signals back into analogue form so that they can be handled by ordinary amplifiers, loudspeakers, etc.

Analogue

An analogue quantity is one that can have absolutely any value. Virtually everything in the 'real world' is analogue — a piece of string can be cut to any length. Much modern electronics deals in digital signals, where only a certain series of values are allowed. A piece of digital string would be one that could be cut to any length provided it was a whole number of (say) metres. Provided a digital system has a high enough resolution (i.e. its minimum increments are small enough) its digital nature will not detract from its performance. In fact the best digital audio circuits now seem able to out-perform the best analogue circuits in most respects.

Baud rate

This is the speed at which data is transmitted in an serial data system (such as MIDI). MIDI operates at 31250 baud (or 31.25 kilobaud), which means that with a continuous stream of data some 31250 bits of information per second are sent. This is not quite as good as it might at first appear, since ten bits (including timing bits) per byte are required,and typically three bytes per MIDI message are needed. This works out at around one thousand MIDI messages per second. This is adequate for most purposes, but with complex systems it is possible for MIDI to become overloaded.

Binary

A form of numbering system where the only digits used are 0 and 1. This may seem a bit crude, but it is the system used in all digital electronics, and MIDI sends values in the form of binary numbers.

Bit

Bit is an abbreviation for 'binary digit', which is the basic unit of information used in a digital system (such as MIDI).

Byte

A set of eight digital bits. Single bits are of little use for most applications, and a set of eight bits is the basic digital building block. The bits are used together to provide a range of values from 0 to 255 (decimal), or 00000000 to 11111111 in binary.

Chain connection
See 'THRU'

Channel messages
These are simply the MIDI messages that carry a channel number in the header byte, and which can therefore be directed to one instrument, or one voice of an instrument. These messages include such things as note on, note off, and program change instructions. Messages that do not contain a channel number are called system messages.

Channel
MIDI can operate on up to sixteen channels that are normally simply called channels 1 to 16. Many MIDI messages carry a channel number, and can be selected by just one instrument (mode 3) or one voice of an instrument (mode 4). Note that any equipment set with 'omni on' will simply ignore channel numbers and respond to all messages.

Chip
A name often used to describe an integrated circuit (which is based on a chip of silicon). These are the components that do most of the work in modern instruments, and permit such advanced designs to be produced in such compact and inexpensive forms.

Clock
A clock signal (in electronic music) is a regular series of electronic pulses sent from one sequencer to another in order to keep the two units properly synchronized (a system which is mainly associated with drum machines). In a MIDI context the clock signal is a regular series of MIDI clock messages, rather than just a simple series of pulses. In a computer a clock is a circuit which provides a regular train of pulses at a very high frequency (usually a few million pulses per second). These pulses move the microprocessor, and hence also the system as a whole, from one operation to the next.

Control voltage (CV)
Analogue synthesizers have as many of their circuits as possible under voltage control. This enables one section of an instrument to modulate another, such as using a low frequency oscillator to modulate a VCO in order to produce the vibrato effect. Any voltage that is used to control a VCO, VCA, etc. is a control voltage. Most analogue synthesizers have a 1 volt per octave CV characteristic.

Controller (1)

MIDI controller messages enable individual controls of an instrument or other piece of MIDI equipment to be adjusted. For example, they can be used to vary the parameters of an ADSR envelope shaper (variable controllers), or to permit the low frequency modulation to be switched on and off (switch controllers).

Controller (2)

A MIDI controller is also any device that transmits MIDI codes, and which can therefore control other MIDI equipment. Originally MIDI controllers were keyboards, but these days there are computer based controllers, foot pedals, guitar controllers, and various other types. You do not have to be a keyboard player in order to exploit the power of MIDI.

Copy protection

This is where a software producer uses some system of data encoding (or whatever) to prevent program disks and tapes from being copied. The idea is to prevent people from copying software bought by their friends rather than buying their own (legitimate) copy. Some disks are copyable, but the copies will not load and run properly. Another method, and one that is popular with the more expensive programs, is to have a 'dongle' or 'security key'. This is an electronic device which connects to one of the computer's ports. 'Dongled' software can be copied, but will not run without the right dongle connected to the computer. The use of copy protection and similar methods by the software publishers is quite understandable. On the other hand, it can be inconvenient to users who are presumably paying any extra costs involved. Many users avoid copy protected software as far as possible, and not due to any dishonest intentions.

Crash

An error ('bug') in a program, or something like interference on the mains supply, can result in a computer crashing. This can manifest itself in a number of ways. The screen may go blank or fill with random characters, the computer may simply freeze-up with the controls having no effect, or you may end up back in the operating system. I have also encountered software that refuses to exit from a command properly, leaving you in an endless loop with no way of getting back into the main body of the program. If a computer crashes, any data not saved to disk will almost certainly be lost.

Decibel

The loudness of sounds is usually measured on a decibel scale. However, decibels can be used in other ways, such as expressing the losses through a filter. Decibels utilize a logarithmic scale.

Delay

Some sequencers have a delay facility, which enables data for one track to be sent slightly delayed relative to data for another track. The idea of this is to permit instruments to be properly synchronized when one responds more rapidly to data than another. This is not an effect I have encountered, but a delay facility is presumably more than a little useful with a system that does suffer from this problem. Significant delays are sometimes introduced (so it is said) when data passes from an IN socket to a THRU socket, but this is again something that I have never encountered. With a large system using the chain method of connection it is corrupted data rather than significant delays that would seem to be the main danger.

Digital

See analogue.

DIN connector

This is the standard type of plug/socket used for MIDI interconnections. Note that it is no good trying to buy any DIN connector, as there are numerous types. The variety used for MIDI interconnections is the 5 way 180 degree type.

Directories

It is often convenient to compartmentalize disks so that data and programs can be stored in several groups, rather than having everything together in one mass of files. This is especially useful with hard disks, which can store massive amounts of data. In fact it is essential to efficient use of hard disks. A common method of organizing things is to have each program in its own 'directory', together with its data. If there is a lot of data associated with a program, then the data can conveniently be stored in a number of sub-directories (one for each month's data for example). Directories and sub-directories do not exist as physically separate parts of the disk. They exist only by virtue of the fact that software sorts the files into the required groups.

Disk (disc)

A computer disk is a device for magnetically storing data (programs, sound samples, songs for a sequencer, etc.), and a disk drive is the hardware that records data onto and reads it back from a disk. Disks enable libraries of data to be built up, and provide a reasonably permanent form of storage (remember that the memories of many instruments and virtually all computers are completely lost when the power is switched off). Cassette recorders are often used as a cheap alternative to disk drives, but are slower and less convenient.

Dot matrix
Dot matrix is a term which is used to describe a certain type of printer. The printhead has a number of minute pins which are repeatedly hammered against the ribbon and paper to produce patterns of dots on the paper. These patterns are the normal alphanumeric characters, but most dot matrix printer are also capable of producing graphic (such as printouts of musical scores). There are other types of printer which use dots to produce text and graphics (e.g. laser printers) but these are not normally considered to be dot matrix printers.

Dynamics
The dynamics of a sound are its changes in volume.

Edit
This is a general computing term which simply means making alterations to data (a word processor document, score in a notation program, or whatever). One of the biggest advantages of computers over conventional methods is the ease with which existing material can be edited, allowing old material to be loaded and altered to suit new requirements, etc.

Event editor
Some sequencers provide facilities for the user to edit any piece of MIDI data. This includes such things as changing note values and durations, and altering velocity values. A good event editor provides the user with tremendous control over the finished piece.

Event
A MIDI event is merely a MIDI message of some kind. Sequencers often have their storage capacity specified as a certain number of events. As note on and note off commands are separate events, and aftertouch or other messages may be involved, the maximum note capacity is likely to be less than half the maximum number of events that can be accommodated.

Expander
An instrument that has no keyboard or other built-in method of playing it. Units of this type are usually controlled from a keyboard

or a computer via a MIDI link. This term was at one time applied to MIDI THRU boxes, but is now little used in this context.

Factory preset

As programming many modern synthesizers is something more than child's play, most synthesizers have a range of ready-programmed sounds available. They can therefore be used by anyone, even if they have little understanding of the instrument. Only using the factory presets means severely under-utilizing most instruments though.

File

In a computer context a 'file' is normally some data, a program, or anything stored on disk as a single entity. Data etc. is stored on disk (or tape) in named files, and most disk systems can handle a hundred or more files per disk provided the files are quite small. It is usually up to the user to provide the file name, and to choose something appropriate so that data can be easily located at some later time.

Filter

A MIDI filter is not an audio filter that is controlled by way of MIDI signals. It is a device that connects into the MIDI cable and blocks certain types of message from its output. For example, a filter could be added ahead of an instrument that only has omni modes and will respond to messages on all channels. By removing all channel messages except those on a particular channel, the instrument could effectively be used in mode 3.

Floppy disk

A floppy disk is an ordinary computer disk, so-called because the disk is made of a thin plastic material which is literally quite floppy (but which is often contained in a rigid plastic casing). Hard disks are, unlike floppy disks, normally non-interchangeable, and are based on a rigid metal disk. They can store far more information than floppy disks, and give much faster access to the data.

Frequency

The pitch of a signal expressed as a frequency in hertz (Hz) rather than as a musical note. Middle A is at 440Hz, which means that there are 440 complete cycles in a one second period.

Glitch

This is a general term which describes a momentary fault in an electronic circuit.

Hard disk (fixed disk)
Normal computer disks are often called 'floppy' disks, as the disk on which magnetic coating is deposited is far from rigid. A hard disk is a more sophisticated type where the disk is rigid, rotates continuously at high speed, and can not be removed from the drive. The non-interchangeability of the disks is not a major drawback, as the capacity of a hard disk is typically equal to that of about 60 floppy disks. The point of a hard disk is that it gives very rapid access to vast amounts of data. An increasingly popular feature on up-market computers, and also to be found on some of the more recent sound samplers.

Hardware
Hardware is simply any piece of electronic equipment, including computers and musical instruments. Data or programs used by the equipment is the 'software'. Data or programs held on ROM are sometimes referred to as 'firmware', presumably because they are a combination of software (the data in the ROM) and hardware (the ROM itself)!

Hertz (Hz)
The unit in which frequency is measured. A frequency of 1 hertz means there is one complete cycle per second. High audio frequencies are usually expressed in kilohertz (kHz). One kilohertz is equal to 1000 hertz.

Hexadecimal (Hex)
Hexadecimal (see Appendix 2) is a system of numbering based on sixteen rather than ten like the ordinary decimal system. The normal numeric digits from 0 to 9 are augmented by the first six letters of the alphabet (A to F) in order to give the sixteen different single digit numbers required by the system. Equipment manuals often give MIDI codes in hexadecimal form, but usually include a conversion table that gives hex to decimal conversions.

Icon
See WIMP.

Kilobyte (K)
The storage capacity of computer disks and memory circuits is often quoted in kilobytes, or just as so many k. A kilobyte is one thousand bytes of data, or, if you wish to be pedantic, 1024 bytes.

LA
LA (linear arithmetic) synthesis is an odd but very effective mixture

of sampled sounds and conventional analogue synthesis techniques. The system used in a number of Roland's synthesizers.

Laser printer
A printer which uses a scanning laser and photocopier technology to produce high quality text and graphics. Some printers use a similar technique, but instead of a laser utilize LED or LCD technology.

Layering
Also known as stacking, this is where two or more voices of an instrument can be played with each key-press. Some very complex sounds can be obtained by layering a multi-timbral instrument, or using several interconnected instruments to obtain the same results.

Librarian
This is a computer program that stores sets of voice data for synthesizers or other instruments. It enables the required sounds to be quickly selected and loaded from disk and transmitted to the instrument via MIDI.

Linear arithmetic
See LA.

Load
If you have some data on disk or tape (a sequence for example) and you wish to recall it for editing or other purposes, you 'load' it into the program. When you run a program you are said to 'load' it from disk or tape into the computer.

Looping
Looping is the process of using the end section of a sample over and over again, so that rather than coming to an abrupt end, the signal is sustained indefinitely. Conventional envelope shaper techniques are normally used to give the signal the desired release characteristic.

Megabyte
The capacity of large memory circuits and high capacity disks is often quoted in megabytes. A megabyte is equivalent to 1024k, or 1048576 bytes.

Microprocessor
This is the component at the heart of a microcomputer. In order to function it needs a lot of other hardware, including memory, input/output ports, power supplies etc. It is the microprocessor

that undertakes the manipulation of data, performs mathematical calculations, and controls everything in the system.

MIDI choke (or clog)

A term used to describe what happens if a system is called upon to transmit more data than MIDI can handle. Exactly what happens when MIDI choke occurs depends on the system, but at the very least it is likely that the timing of note on/off messages will be severely disrupted. In an extreme case it is possible that the MIDI controller would crash, and the system would be brought to a halt.

MIDI

MIDI stands for 'musical instrument digital interface'. It is a means of controlling one instrument for another, or controlling an instrument from a computer. MIDI is a very versatile and capable system of interfacing suitably equipped musical instruments (see *Practical MIDI Handbook* from the publishers of this book for a full explanation of MIDI).

Mod-wheel

A modulation wheel is present on most synthesizers. It is usually a large edge-type rotary control that is used to adjust the modulation depth provided by the LFO.

MODEM

This name is a contraction of MODulator/DEModulator. A modem is a device that enables computers to communicate via the ordinary telephone system. In order to do this a modem converts serial signals into a two tone audio signal (one tone for each logic level). There are a number of tone standards in operation, and you need the right kind of modem (or a multi-standard type) in order to be certain of correct data transfer between your computer and another system.

Modifier

Any device which acts on and alters a signal in some way.

Mono

In a MIDI context 'mono' means that only one note per channel is possible. In MIDI mode 2 an instrument is truly monophonic as operation on only one channel is possible, but in mode 4 (formerly known as mono mode) it is possible for an instrument to operate monophonically on several channels. The instrument is then polyphonic, while it is the MIDI channels that are monophonic. The term 'mono' is perhaps a bit misleading in this respect.

Mouse
See WIMP.

Notation program
Also called 'score writer' programs, these permit music to be written into the computer in standard music notation form. Some programs of this type are simply intended as a means of producing sheet music, but many now support MIDI, and will operate as step-time sequencers. In fact some will turn MIDI data into notes on the staves and will operate as real-time sequencers (but will not necessarily work particularly well in this role).

Null MODEM
Null modem is normally used to describe a type of cable for connecting RS232C serial interfaces together. It has crossed-over wires that enable it to connect together two interfaces of the same type. This is the type of cable you will normally need for interconnecting two RS232C serial ports.

Omni
When 'omni' is 'on', an instrument will respond to messages on any MIDI channel. When omni is off, the instrument will only respond to one particular channel (modes 2 and 3), or each voice will be assigned to a particular channel (mode 4).

Opto-isolator
This is an electronic component that consists of a LED having its output directed at a photocell, with both components contained in an opaque case. This enables a signal to be coupled from one circuit to another without any electrical connection between them. All MIDI inputs are opto-isolated, and amongst other things this helps to minimize problems with hum loops.

Oscillator
An oscillator is the electronic equivalent of the resonator (such as a reed) in an acoustic instrument. It generates a signal of the required waveform, although only some simple wave shapes (triangle, sine, square, etc.) are easily generated. Complex waveforms are generated using several oscillators plus (possibly) filtering, or using a DCO.

Parameter
Anything on a synthesizer that can be adjusted (envelope rates and levels, filter frequencies, etc.) is a parameter.

156

Parity
Parity checking is used by some serial interfaces as a simple means of error checking. Either an even number of 1s (even parity) or an odd number of 1s (odd parity) are present in every block of data, with the system adding extra 1s where necessary in order to give the correct parity. A simple checking circuit at the receiving end of the system detects the error if the wrong number of 1s are present in a block of data, and also strips off the added bits to give just the required bytes of data. Parity is not much used in practice, and can easily miss corrupted bytes of data. A form of parity checking is also used in the memory circuits of some computers (notably the IBM PCs and compatibles). They consequently need nine memory chips in order to store eight bit bytes of data.

Patch
A patch is a method of interconnecting the various parts of a synthesizer. It dates back to the modular synthesizer days when the instrument was wired up in the required manner using patch leads which connected to sockets on the front panel of the instrument.

Phase
This is a term that is mostly used when describing one waveform's relationship to another. A complete cycle has the wave going through 360 degrees (180 degrees on the first half cycle, and then 180 degrees in the opposite direction on the second one). If one wave is half a cycle behind another one, it would therefore be said to be phase lagging it by 180 degrees.

Pointer
In the sense of a song pointer, it is a MIDI message that moves a sequencer to a certain point in the sequence. As a computing term it means an on screen pointer (see WIMP).

Poly
In polyphonic mode an instrument can handle several notes at once. In the case of mode 3 it is possible to have polyphonic operation on each MIDI channel. The maximum number of notes available at one time is determined by the instruments — the MIDI specification does not set any upper limit.

Port
A port is merely some form of electrical connector on a computer or other piece of electronics to enable it to be connected to some

peripheral device. MIDI IN, OUT, and THRU sockets are all examples of ports. The alternative term interface is sometimes used.

Preset

A term that can be applied to any set of parameters that are preprogrammed and can be quickly called up when needed. It normally describes a set of parameters that give a certain sound. The required sound can be selected by pushing a button or two, and with most synthesizers there are dozens of presets loaded and available almost instantly.

Pressure sensitive

Touch sensitive keyboards generally use the speed with which a key is depressed to control the peak volume on the attack phase of the envelope. A pressure sensitive type will also use the key pressure to control the volume after the attack phase (usually on the sustain phase). The key pressure may also be used to control other parameters, particularly those of the VCF (or equivalent circuit).

Printout

Some programs enable data to be printed via a suitable printer. This is very useful, especially with something like a sequencer program that permits only a small portion of long sequences to be displayed on the screen. Also useful with notation (score writer) programs where it enables conventional sheet music to be produced. However, for graphics output a graphics compatible printer is needed (most programs will work properly with any Epson compatible dot-matrix printer).

Program

This is a term which has several meanings, but in a synthesizer context it normally refers to a set of sound data. In other words it is much the same as a preset. In a computer context it means a piece of software, such as a sequencer or a word processor.

Program change

Most instruments and other item of MIDI equipment make use of 'programs'. In an instrument for example, these are a series of preset control settings that give a range of different sounds. Program change messages therefore permit the required sounds to be selected at the appropriate times. Note that other items of MIDI equipment such as mixers and effects units are often controlled via program change messages.

Program dump
Many MIDI equipped instruments have the ability to send out via MIDI the full contents of their program memory, or to provide a 'program dump'. This can be used to send a set of programs from one instrument to another (but they will normally need to be instruments of exactly the same type). This facility can also be used to send data to a computer or MIDI disk drive, and then feed it back again when and as required. There is no special MIDI program dump message, and this facility operates under system exclusive messages.

Pulse
A pulse waveform is generally accepted as one where the signal is either at a high negative level, or a high positive one, and it switches rapidly from one to the other. A squarewave is a form of pulse signal, but a triangular wave, due to its gradual change from one peak level to the other, is not. Any brief and intermittent waveform tends to be called a pulse signal, regardless of its exact shape.

Quickdisk
This is a disk of a similar type to those used to store computer data. However, at 2.8 inches in diameter a Quickdisk does not conform to any computer standard, and these disks only seem to be used with samplers. Most samplers now seem to use standard 3.5 inch computer disks which are cheaper, tougher, and have a much higher capacity. This second point is important with the large memory capacities of many modern samplers. It can take both sides of several Quickdisks to fully load a sampler with even quite modest amounts of memory.

Qwerty keyboard
A term which seems to confuse a lot of people, it simply refers to a typewriter style keyboard (as used in expanded form on virtually all computers). QWERTY are the first six letters on the top row of letters keys.

RAM
This is the type of memory used in samplers to store the sample data. The electronics in the system can write data into this 'random access memory', unlike ROM (read only memory) which must be programmed at the manufacturing stage. ROM retains its contents indefinitely, but RAM loses the data it contains when the power is switched off. Disks are used to magnetically store samples where long-term storage is required (which it normally will be). Small

amounts of RAM can be battery-backed. This means having a battery which maintains power to the RAM when the unit is switched off. The battery typically lasts about five years. Many synthesizers hold data for their preset sounds in RAM, and use this system of battery back-up.

Real-time sequencer
A sequencer where the music is entered into the unit simply by playing it on a MIDI keyboard. The sequencer records the data from the keyboard, which is stored in its memory together with timing information. The ability to change the playback speed is a standard feature. The more up-market systems permit note values and durations to be edited, and multi-track sequences to be built up.

ROM
ROM stands for 'read only memory'. As this name suggests, once the contents of ROM have been set at the manufacturing stage they can not be altered. The main point about ROM is that it retains its contents when the power is switched off (unlike ordinary RAM). ROM is used for storing data and (or) programs that will be needed frequently. RAM (see above) is what is needed for storing your own data and programs.

Root directory
When a computer disk is divided into directories and subdirectories, a default directory is entered when the disk is first used. This is the root directory, and all the others branch out from this directory, either directly or from the directories and sub-directories that have their origins in the root directory.

RS232C
This is the standard form of serial port which is fitted to many computers and peripherals as standard, and is almost invariably available as an extra where it is not fitted. It transfers data one bit at a time rather than on a byte by byte basis, which makes it a relatively slow form of interface. Quite long ranges can be accommodated though. The RS423 interface fitted to some computers is compatible with the RS232C type.

RS422
An RS422 port is a form of serial interface. It is more sophisticated than the more common RS232C type in that it uses a balanced line connection (i.e. two signal wires) rather than the more common one signal wire plus earth connection. It can achieve faster transfer

rates and longer range than the RS232C type. It is mainly used on quite expensive professional equipment.

Sampling
This is a form of digital recording and playback. Sounds are recorded into the instrument and stored in RAM. They are then played back at the desired pitch. This gives some very convincing acoustic instrument sounds, but a lot of weird and wonderful sounds can also be produced by sampling non-instrument sounds. Many samplers have complex VCFs, VCAs, envelope generators, LFOs and modulation sections, etc. This gives plenty of scope for modifying recorded sounds, and most samplers are considerably more just than recording and playback devices.

Save
When you switch off a computer the entire contents of its memory are normally lost. To avoid data being lost forever, it is 'saved' to disk or tape before switching off the computer. You might also save data before clearing the computer's memory and going on to a fresh piece of work. When you need to use saved data again you 'load' it back into the computer.

Serial
MIDI is a form of serial communications system, which simply means that it sends information one 'bit' at a time. Parallel systems send data several 'bits' at a time, and are usually much faster. They need multi-way connecting cables though, and often have very restricted ranges (a couple of metres in some cases). Although slower, a serial system is more practical for many applications.

Software
Software originally meant computer programs in any form (on disk, tape, written down, or whatever). It seems to be more generalized these days, and sound samples for use in a sound sampler would now be considered 'software'.

Star connection
See THRU box.

Step-time sequencer
This is a sequencer where the music is programmed by specifying the note value and duration in some way other than playing the music onto a MIDI keyboard and recording the MIDI output data plus timing information. A notation program where the music is placed onto an on-screen stave (or staves) in conventional music notation form is an up-market example of a step-time sequencer.

With more simple types the notes are entered in a more simple form, such as 'C-2, 1/4 note' for instance. Great if your imagination out-performs your playing skills, but a relatively slow way of doing things.

Sustain pedal

Many synthesizers have a socket for a sustain pedal. This give an effect which is similar to that of a piano's sustain pedal. Notes have an extended release period, unless the instrument runs out of voices that is. Existing notes are then normally terminated to make way for the new ones.

System messages

These are the MIDI message that do not carry a channel number in the header byte. They are therefore responded to by every piece of equipment in the system that recognizes them. These are mainly the MIDI clock and associated messages.

System exclusive

The system exclusive messages are ones that are designed for use only by equipment from one manufacturer. The header byte includes an identification number so that system exclusive messages from equipment of the wrong manufacturer can be filtered out and ignored. Virtually any feature can be implemented using system exclusive messages, and unlimited data can be included in each one of these!

THRU

A THRU socket is to be found on many items of MIDI equipment. It simply provides a replica of what is received on the IN socket. In a multi-unit system the THRU socket on one unit can be coupled through to the IN socket of the next unit (chain connection).

THRU box

Not all MIDI units have THRU sockets, and in particular, they are often absent from keyboard instruments. A THRU box has a MIDI IN socket and several THRU output sockets. In a multi-unit system the OUT socket of the controller connects to the IN socket of the THRU box. The THRU outputs then connect to the IN socket of each instrument etc. in the system (star connection).

Timbre

The characteristics of sounds that distinguish one instrument from another. Timbre is mainly governed by the harmonic content and envelope of a signal. It is these differences in timbre that result in one instrument sounding very different to another playing the same note.

Touch sensitive
This applies to a keyboard that provides velocity information to the synthesizer. This information is normally used to control the volume of each note, so that playing the keyboard hard gives increased volume. The velocity information often controls the filtering as well. A good touch sensitive keyboard will also implement aftertouch.

Track
In a MIDI context, 'track' is a term used in sequencing. Virtually all sequencers allow music to be built up track-by-track, as in multi-track tape recording. In a computing context, it is a term which pertains to disks. Information is stored on computer disks in a number of concentric tracks (usually 40 or 80 of them on each side of the disk).

Tree
This is a disk term, but not all disk operating systems support directory trees. This is where you effectively separate a disk into a number of sections, or 'sub-directories' as they are termed. If there are a large number of files on a disk it can make things more manageable if they are placed in two or more (effectively) separate sections of the disk. If a very large number of files are involved, sub-directories of sub-directories can be used to further compart-mentalize the disk. A 'tree' is a diagram or chart which shows the sub-directories present on a disk, and the way in which they branch out from one another.

Velocity sensitive
This term is applied to a keyboard instrument which responds to the hardness with which the keys are played. The harder keys are operated, the louder notes are played (like many acoustic keyboard instruments).

Visual editor
A program for use with sound samplers, it draws out waveforms on the screen so that suitable start, end and loop points can be selected quickly and accurately. Relies on swopping sound sample information via MIDI system exclusive messages.

Voice editor
The minimalist approach to synthesizer controls has made setting up the required sounds a relatively long and difficult process. A voice editor program provides on-screen controls that can quickly and easily be adjusted. New controls settings are almost instantly sent to the instrument via MIDI so that the effect of adjusting controls can be heard, and fine adjustments easily made.

Voltage control

It is voltage control that largely distinguishes synthesizers from other instruments. The main point about having everything, as far as possible, under voltage control, is that it enables virtually any part of the instrument to control virtually any other part. This permits complex modulation to be used, and equally complex sounds to be generated.

WIMP

WIMP is an acronym for 'Windows, Icons, Mouse, and Pointer'. It is a means of controlling computer programs, where an on screen pointer is moved around the screen using a hand operated controller (the 'mouse'). The mouse and pointer are used to select options via 'icons', which are on-screen graphical representations (pictures of various instruments so you can select the one you wish to use for example). The 'windows' are areas of the screen which are given over to different functions, or with some computers can even be used for different programs! A WIMP environment makes it easy for inexperienced users to operate complex programs, but only if the software is well designed and the computer is powerful enough to run it properly.

Window

See 'WIMP'.

Word

In a computer sense, this is a group of bits that is longer than a normal 8 bit byte. For example, with a sixteen bit sound sampler, a memory capacity of 500 k words means that 500 k of full 16 bit words can be accommodated (which is equivalent to 1000 k bytes of storage).

XLR

This is a type of electrical connector used for MIDI interconnections on some equipment (generally units that are designed for rough handling 'on the road'). Any supplier of MIDI equipment which uses this type of connector should be able to supply suitable connecting leads as well, together with adaptors to permit standard 5 way DIN MIDI leads to be used.

Appendix 2
Hexadecimal numbers

Something in the MIDI sections of equipment manuals that can cause confusion to the uninitiated is the use of hexadecimal ('hex') numbers. These are used a great deal in computing as they are more compact than binary numbers, but are easily converted into binary equivalents. Decimal numbers are compact, although a little less so than hexadecimal numbers, but are not so easily converted into binary. The MIDI user, unless he or she is into designing his or her own hardware, is not likely to need to use binary numbers at all. You may need to convert from hexadecimal to decimal, since you might need to enter values into a program in decimal form, whereas the manual which gives the values you require might work in hexadeximal.

Whereas the decimal system is based on the number ten, with ten single digit numbers from 0 to 9, hexadecimal is based on the number sixteen, and has sixteen single digit numbers. Obviously the decimal system has too few numeric characters to accommodate the hexadecimal system. This problem is easily rectified by augmenting the ten normal numbers with the first six letters of the alphabet (A to F). It is from this that the term 'hexadecimal' is derived. Single digit hexadecimal numbers therefore run from 0 to F. The number 10 in hexadecimal is equivalent to 16 in decimal (i.e. it is one sixteen and no units). Byte size numbers can be accommodated by hexadecimal numbers only two digits long. You do not need to be a mathematical genius in order to do hexadecimal to decimal conversion, but it is quicker and easier to simply use a conversion chart such as the one shown below.

Hexadecimal numbers

	0	1	2	3	4	5	6	7	8	9	A	B	C	D	E	F
0	0	1	2	3	4	5	6	7	8	9	10	11	12	13	14	15
1	16	17	18	19	20	21	22	23	24	25	26	27	28	29	30	31
2	32	33	34	35	36	37	38	39	40	41	42	43	44	45	46	47
3	48	49	50	51	52	53	54	55	56	57	58	59	60	61	62	63
4	64	65	66	67	68	69	70	71	72	73	74	75	76	77	78	79
5	80	81	82	83	84	85	86	87	88	89	90	91	92	93	94	95
6	96	97	98	99	100	101	102	103	104	105	106	107	108	109	110	111
7	112	113	114	115	116	117	118	119	120	121	122	123	124	125	126	127
8	128	129	130	131	132	133	134	135	136	137	138	139	140	141	142	143
9	144	145	146	147	148	149	150	151	152	153	154	155	156	157	158	159
A	160	161	162	163	164	165	166	167	168	169	170	171	172	173	174	175
B	176	177	178	179	180	181	182	183	184	185	186	187	188	189	190	191
C	192	193	194	195	196	197	198	199	200	201	202	203	204	205	206	207
D	208	209	210	211	212	213	214	215	216	217	218	219	220	221	222	223
E	224	225	226	227	228	229	230	231	232	233	234	235	236	237	238	239
F	240	241	242	243	244	245	246	247	248	249	250	251	252	253	254	255

As an example of how this conversion chart is used, suppose that you want to convert the hexadecimal number C5 to its decimal equivalent. The first digit (C in this case) is located in the left hand column. Then go across to the column headed by the second digit, which is 5 in this instance. You then simply read of the answer, which for our example of C5 is 197.

Of course, it is just as easy to use the chart the other way round to provide decimal to hexadecimal conversion. Simply find the decimal number in the main body of the chart, then read off the first hexadecimal digit from the row heading for that number, and the second hexadecimal number from the column heading. For instance, 99 has 6 as its row heading, and 3 as its column heading, giving a hexadecimal answer of 63.

Appendix 3
Checklists

If you are buying a computer, printer, synth/sampler, sequencer software or notation program, you will no doubt be bewildered by the wide range of goods on offer. The following checklists cover the features that are of special interest if you are going to set up a computer-based music making system.

Printers

1. Graphics capability (Epson FX or LQ compatible for a dot matrix machine, HP Laserjet or Postscript compatible in the case of page printer). Not a daisywheel type (little or no graphics capability).
2. Reasonably fast print speed (150 cps or more draft, 50 cps or more in LQ or NLQ).
3. Good print quality, with no faint or over-inked areas of print (can only be determined from a subjective assessment of sample printouts).
4. Easy to load the paper and set up ready for use. Should ideally have tractor feed for continuous stationery as standard.
5. The ability to easily change from continuous to single sheet stationery (some machines allow the use of single sheets without removing the continuous stationery).
6. An automatic sheet feeder if you will only use single sheets of paper. This is standard on most page printers (e.g. laser printers) which do not take continuous stationery, but can be an expensive add on for dot matrix machines).
7. Inexpensive and long lasting consumables (page printers can be expensive to run, as can some dot matrix types which have expensive and short lived ribbons).

8. Parallel and serial interfaces as standard, for optimum interfacing flexibility (or failing that a built-in parallel port with a serial port available as a reasonably low cost add-on).

Less important features

1. Build quality. Heavy duty printers are much more expensive, and you are unlikely to give them enough use to justify this added cost.
2. Large buffer.

Computers

1. Good screen graphics resolution (preferably about 640 × 350 or better). Colour is an advantage, but not crucial for music applications.
2. Mouse as standard (saves the additional cost of buying one, and any software which can usefully utilize the mouse will probably do so).
3. Good software base. Do not buy any computer unless you are sure that the applications software you will wish to run on it is actually available for that particular machine.
4. Good quality keyboard. The best software in the world will be a pain to use on a computer with a poor quality keyboard.
5. Plenty of standard ports. Standard parallel, serial, monitor ports, etc. gives you a wide range of choice when you wish to add a peripheral device to the system. Few or non-standard ports limit the options and make upgrading the system expensive.
6. Built-in floppy disk drive or drives. It is difficult to do any serious computing without at least one disk drive.
7. Hard disk drive. Will transform the performance of some complex software (but not worth the high cost if your programs run all right from a floppy disk).
8. 16 bit processor. Many music applications require a lot of processing power, giving 16 bit computers a definite advantage over 8 bit types.
9. Large memory (preferably at least 1M). The complexity of many music programs means that they gobble up large amounts of memory. Some will not run on anything less than a megabyte!
10. MIDI interface (either built-in or available as a low cost add-on).

Less important features

1. Free software etc. (you may as well have any freebies that are on offer, but a lower price without the free bits and pieces is often a better deal).

Synthesizers/samplers

1. Quality of the sounds. If you do not like the sounds, you will not like the results regardless of the instrument's capabilities in other respects.
2. MIDI Mode 4. If you want to use a lot of sounds at once, one mode 4 instrument is a lot cheaper than several in mode 3.
3. Multi mode. The monophonic operation of mode 4 can be very restrictive, and the polyphonic operation provided by a multi mode of some kind is a great advantage.
4. About 32 note polyphony. Together with multi mode and (preferably) dynamic note allocation, this gives what is genuinely an instrument with the power of about half a dozen synthesizers.
5. Large memory so that a large number of sounds can be stored 'on-board'.
6. Non-volatile memory so that when the instrument is switched on it takes up where it left off at the end of the last session.
7. Disk drive. For samplers or other instruments where non-volatile memory is not feasible, a built-in disk drive for rapid loading of data is nearly as good.
8. A rack-mount version. Keyboards are expensive, take up a lot of space, and you will probably only need one in the system. Rack-mount units are the most practical way of expanding a music system.
9. Graphics display. A graphics display can make it much easier to adjust sounds, or get the looping right in the case of a sound sampler.
10. Good quality keyboard. At least one instrument in the system should have a good quality keyboard, preferably covering five octaves or more, with velocity sensitivity. Some form of aftertouch is an advantage these days.
11. A full set of MIDI sockets (the THRU socket is not included on all MIDI instruments).
12. The availability of a programmer unit (or voice editor software for your computer). Setting up your own sounds without one of these could be a long, difficult and tedious task.

13. Large range of built-in or ready sampled/programmed sounds available. Too much setting up of your own sounds can leave little time for using the instrument!

Less important features

1. Built-in sequencer. If you will be using a computer-based sequencer to control the instrument via MIDI, any built-in sequencer is unlikely to get used.

Sequencer software

1. Plenty of tracks. Obviously depends on the type of music you will be producing and the instruments you have, but you can soon outgrow sixteen tracks.
2. Add-on multiple MIDI interface. To make full use of a large number of tracks you will need the ability to direct each one to a different channel, which requires more than one MIDI OUT for more than sixteen tracks.
3. Event editor. In order to unleash the full power of MIDI you need the ability to change data at event level. Even a crude event editor is a great asset.
4. The ability to load data from other sequencers (many ST sequencers now have the ability to save and load data in a standardized format).
5. Usable quantization. Simple quantization can be counter-productive. Ideally several forms of sophisticated quantization should be on offer.
6. Notation display, player piano display, or some other convenient means of step-time sequencing.
7. Drum tracks facility. The ability to repeat a short sequence a number of times so that drum tracks can be rapidly created (an alternative to using a drum machine's built-in sequencer).
8. An 'undo' facility. If you make a drastic mistake, it puts everything back the way it was.
9. The ability to mass process data (multiply all velocity values by X for example).
10. Comprehensive and controllable MIDI filtering on both transmitted and received data.

Notation programs

1. The ability to handle up to at least sixteen staves.
2. Compatible with a wide variety of printers, and should as a minimum have high density Epson FX and LQ compatible output.
3. Able to read in data from at least one sequencer (or total integration with a sequencer program).
4. Large range of symbols available, preferably with the ability to draw your own.
5. Full range of key signatures, note values, time signatures, etc.
6. The ability to play scores via MIDI, rather than simply operating as a note processor.
7. An even editor to permit 'fine tuning' of the MIDI data.
8. Comprehensive copying facilities, including copying from one stave to another.
9. A transpose feature (so that transposing instruments can have the correct notation display, but will still play the right notes over MIDI).
10. Diagonal rather than horizontal 'beams' (gives a more professional printed output, but diagonal lines do not print very neatly on many printers).

Appendix 4: MIDI controller allocations

Control no.	Function
1	Modulation wheel
2	Breath controller
4	Foot controller
5	Portamento time
6	Data entry (MSB)
7	Main volume
8	Balance
10	Pan
11	Expression controller
16–19	General controllers 1 to 4
32–63	LSB for controllers 0 to 31
64	Sustain pedal
65	Portamento
66	Sostenuto
67	Soft pedal
69	Hold 2
80–83	General controllers 5 to 8
91–95	Effects depth controllers
96	Data increment
97	Data decrement
98	Non-registered parameter No. LSB
99	Non-registered parameter No. MSB
100	Registered parameter No. LSB
101	Registered parameter No. MSB
121–127	Reserved for mode messages

Controller numbers not listed are undefined.

Index

Index